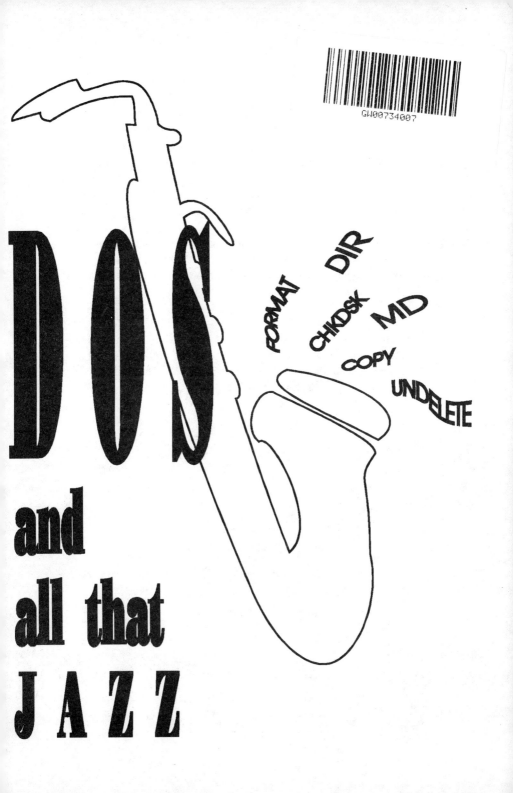

GW00734007

DOS
and
all that
JAZZ

FORMAT DIR CHKDSK MD COPY UNDELETE

First published in April 1992 by
Computer Step, 14 Boleyn Close, Warwick CV34 6LP
Tel. 0926 887366 Fax. 0926 887363

Printed in England by
Clay Special Products, St Ives Plc

All trademarks acknowledged

ISBN 1 874029 01 6

For
Sevanti

About the Author

Harshad Kotecha graduated in Computer Studies in 1983. Since then, he has worked in the computer industry at various levels. His work has included presenting the benefits of using particular computer systems in large organisations and providing training to individuals.

He is also the author of the popular "The PC Novice's Handbook" and several computer user manuals.

Preface

Since its inception, DOS has become the *de facto* operating system for most personal computers. Over the period it has been greatly enhanced to meet the ever increasing needs of hardware and software technologies, as well as user demands. With the release of each version, DOS has become more sophisticated, and still continues to perplex both newcomers and active PC users.

Despite this power and complexity, learning to use DOS should not be a daunting task. This book explains the power of DOS without the complexity.

DOS and all that Jazz is unique:

It is a complete guide for beginners and current users. Whether you have just bought your first PC and never had to learn DOS before, or you are familiar with DOS but need to update your knowledge on the latest version, this book will help you master DOS quickly. If you have an older version of DOS, you can read this book to decide whether it is worth upgrading to version 5.

It teaches you DOS, regardless of the version you have. New DOS 5 features are highlighted and there is a useful section at the back listing DOS commands together with the version number they first appeared in. DOS is upward compatible. This means that DOS commands are valid for the version they first appeared in, and for all subsequent versions.

You will find this book an easy source of reference, even after you upgrade to future versions of DOS, like DOS 6.0, for example. Everything you learn here will still apply because of this upward compatibility.

It caters for users who prefer to use the DOS Shell and for those who are used to working from the Command Prompt. The DOS Shell provides a new easy way to use common functions within DOS. These functions and other more complex ones, not provided within the Shell, can also be typed at the Command Prompt. Both methods of working are covered in this book.

How to use this book

You can read this book from start to finish to get a complete appreciation of DOS. Alternatively, you can refer to specific chapters which may be of interest to you. Of course, the best way to learn DOS is by actually using it. When you read about various commands and features in this book, try them out on your own PC.

If you have an older version of DOS, or you simply prefer not to use the Shell, pay particular attention to the boxed sections. These refer to commands that can be issued from the Command Prompt. For example:

```
From the Command Prompt

    DIR

```

If you have DOS 5 and you only want to learn the common functions that can be performed via the Shell, you can ignore text which is boxed. Some functions, however, cannot be performed via the Shell. If these are important to you, you will have to type them at the DOS Command Prompt.

Commands that you are required to type and the output displayed by your computer will appear in this typeface:

```
This is the computer typeface
```

Commands that were introduced in DOS 5 are highlighted by:

Keys that are used in combination are represented with a hyphen in between. For example,

Alt-F

The above implies that you should press and hold down the Alt key, then tap the 'F' key once.

If you have DOS 5 and it is not installed yet, refer to Appendix A. Install the software before you start following examples in this book.

MISTAKE   P. 40

Table of Contents

Introduction

Dos interacts with, and controls many components on your PC. Therefore, it is important to know the basic workings of your computer before you seriously look at DOS. If you already know about the different parts making up a PC, skip the first section. However, newcomers may like to familiarise themselves quickly with the basic terminology, before diving into DOS.

Essential Beginnings

A computer system consists of hardware and software. Neither can function without the other. Software consists of encoded instructions. Hardware refers to the physical elements, and the important ones are the keyboard, the monitor and the system unit. The keyboard (as well as the mouse) is the main way of 'talking' to the computer. The monitor or the screen is the main device for the computer to output information or to 'talk-back'.

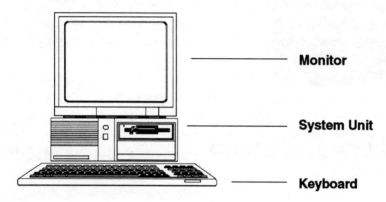

Monitor

System Unit

Keyboard

The System Unit incorporates:

> Micro-processor
> Memory
> Hard Disk
> Floppy Disk Drives

The micro-processor is the 'brain' of the computer. It obeys and processes instructions given to it by programs (or software). It is the processor that performs all functions required of a computer system.

Memory (the most common type is called RAM - *Random Access Memory*) is temporary storage medium inside the computer, to store programs and data. It is used to store information you are working on at the time. Once you switch off the PC, the contents of the RAM is wiped off.

To overcome this limitation, as well as to store large amounts of data, you need a more permanent storage medium. This is offered by hard disks and floppy disks. There is a whole chapter discussing these disks in detail, later in the book.

A disk can be thought of as a filing cabinet, allowing you to store several documents or files. A document, like a letter, report or even a memo is a basic unit of information. A group of related files, like all letters to your Bank Manager, will be kept in the same filing drawer. This in computer terms is a directory, containing files. This directory may be called BANKLTRS. You can have a directory within another directory (sub-directory) to logically organise all your files. Just in the same way as you would divide your filing drawer into sections. So, your BANKLTRS may be within a directory called FINANCE.

If you are not familiar with the main keys on your keyboard, then here is a brief run-down:

Enter. After you have typed a command from your keyboard press this key to send it to the computer. It is also used as a 'carriage return' on a typewriter to mark the end of a paragraph.

Ctrl or **Alt.** These stand for Control or Alternative keys respectively. They are usually used with other keys to perform functions controlled by software.

Function keys. These are usually found along the top of the keyboard, labelled F1 to F12. They are again programmed to perform certain tasks depending on the software you are using. F1, for example will usually provide help in using the system.

Esc. Short for Escape, this key is usually used to cancel or back-out from a screen or option you have chosen. It is located at the top left-hand side of the keyboard.

Arrow keys. There are four keys near the right side of the keyboard used to move the cursor to the left, right, up or down. A cursor is just a pointer displayed on the screen, telling you where the next bit of text you type will appear.

In addition to these, you also have keys, commonly used for word processing, like the Shift, Backspace, Tab, Page Up, Page Down, Insert and Delete.

What is DOS?

DOS is the most important software for the IBM personal computer (PC) or compatibles. It stands for Disk Operating System. Like any other computer operating system, DOS controls all activities on your computer. It decides where in memory to load your programs, transfers files from the hard disk to memory, accepts data from the keyboard, displays information on the screen, handles printing and so on.

We often take DOS for granted because we cannot see exactly what it is doing. Most of the time its activities are transparent to us. For example, when you are using a word processor on your PC and you decide to print a letter, your word processor program has to ask DOS for help (technical jargon is *makes a system call*). Now, it is easy to be fooled into thinking that the word processor program is communicating directly with the printer.

DOS also allows you to interact with it directly. It will accept instructions from you (the operator) and act on them. You can think of DOS as your personal attendant. By learning DOS, you'll be able to organise and manage the information in your computer and use it more easily. We will be looking at most of these features in this book. DOS also provides utilities, like the editor, which are software products in their own right.

DOS Versions

Although we use the term DOS, strictly speaking there are two separate types, called: MS-DOS and PC-DOS. They are both developed by Microsoft Corporation, a leading software company.

PC-DOS was developed specifically for the IBM PC. Microsoft still owns PC-DOS, but it earns large amounts of royalty fees from IBM. MS-DOS is very similar to PC-DOS, but Microsoft sells this to companies producing IBM-compatibles (clone makers). The two versions had to be very similar for the clone makers to have compatibility with the original IBM PC. This has resulted in an explosion of clone makers. There are hundreds of different types of IBM-compatible machines in the market today, all using and running MS-DOS.

Since PC-DOS and MS-DOS are very similar, we will simply use the generic term DOS to refer to both of them. In this book, however, MS-DOS is covered. This is now, by far, the more popular version of DOS.

MS-DOS version 5.0 is the current major release. Note that the decimal digits are important in version numbers. As with any other software version number, an increase in the first decimal digit represents a minor but important upgrade to the package. For example, DOS 3.2 enhanced the product with a few improvements not present in the previous DOS 3.1.

An increase in the second decimal digit represents a very minor improvement. For example, there is virtually no difference between DOS 4.01 and DOS 4.00. Quite often, it is a software bug resolved or something that really should have been implemented in the original version. These upgrades are not usually planned by software companies but have become necessary to rectify errors in the software.

Finally, a change in the main version number, is planned by software companies and represents a major upgrade. Quite often this change is the result of a total rewrite of the software package. At other times, a major upgrade will have substantial changes. For example, DOS 5.0 is a major upgrade from DOS 4.2.

Let us now briefly trace the history of DOS and its versions. DOS 1.00 was born at the same time as the IBM PC - in 1981. This version is now very obsolete and no one uses it. It cannot work with hard disks. It can't even use 360 kilobyte 5.25" floppy disks. Although DOS 1.00 only appeared just over a decade ago, in the software business, this represents a lifetime.

DOS 2.xx became very popular because it supported hard disks as well as 360K 5.25" floppy disks. Even today, many applications support this version of DOS.

DOS 3.xx allowed us to use 3.50" floppy disks for the first time. It also supported high density floppy disks and networks.

DOS 4.xx paved the way for very high capacity hard disks and the Shell. The latter is a high level menu system which makes it easy to use DOS with a mouse.

DOS 5.xx improved memory management so that you have more memory available for your applications. Also, it is now possible to have several applications in memory at the same time, and to swap between them.

Getting Started

hen you switch ON your PC, you will hear the noise of the internal cooling fan, taking air from the front of the PC and pushing it back. Ensure that your PC has enough room at the back for this ventilation. It should not be pressed right against the wall.

Then, you may see a flash of text displayed on the top right-hand side of the screen. This is usually a copyright message or a name of a brand product already installed, with its version number. For example, it may be the type of graphics card your PC uses, like:

ORCHID TECHNOLOGY
Prodesigner IIs BIOS Version 1.1
Advanced Video Graphics Array

For the next few seconds, the PC will appear not to be doing anything. During this time it is checking all its internal parts, including the memory. The memory-test part is important - you may see on your screen, a series of numeric digits rapidly increasing in value as this test is being performed. Usually, these self-tests should not report errors. If you should however, at any time encounter an error, make a note of the error code or message and contact your supplier immediately.

Next, your PC will try to find DOS. It checks drive A first - you may notice the light for drive A come ON momentarily. Although nowadays most of us have DOS installed on drive C (hard disk), early PCs did not have a hard disk and DOS had to be loaded from drive A. For this historic reason and to be upward compatible, drive A is still searched first. If DOS is not found here, then drive C will be accessed and searched. If DOS is not found here either, then you will get a message to that effect and you will be required to insert the DOS disk (sometimes also referred to as the *system disk*) before continuing.

Assuming DOS is found, it is loaded automatically into memory. In this respect, DOS is a software product like any other application software products, including Dbase, Lotus 1-2-3 or WordPerfect. The whole process described above, leading up to loading DOS is often referred to as *booting up*. You can force this same chain of events by pressing Ctrl-Alt-Del keys together or pressing the RESET button found on many personal computers. Be careful though, because when you boot-up, everything in memory (or RAM to be precise) will be lost.

Once DOS is loaded, you will either see the Shell or the Command Prompt depending on how DOS has been set-up on your system.

Command Prompt

When your PC is waiting for your instructions or commands, it will display what is called a Command Prompt on the screen (sometimes also called the System Prompt or the DOS Prompt). It looks like:

The letter C is the current disk drive. It can be A or B, if you log on to one of these floppy disk drives. Drive C is usually the hard disk. It is also the default drive when you power up. Sometimes you can use drive D if you have a second hard disk installed. Other letters are not really used unless your PC is linked to a network.

The greater-than symbol (or >) just tells you that this is where you should type your DOS commands. The small flashing dash after it, is called a cursor. This is where the first character you type will appear. The cursor will also move to the right automatically, ready to receive the next character, and so on. This invisible line where DOS commands are typed is referred to as the *Command Line*. Try typing something on the command line. For example:

        C> COMPUTER STEP

If you have made a mistake in typing or you have changed your mind, press the backspace key to delete characters to the left. The back arrow key too can be used to delete text. You will notice characters disappearing one at a time from the right.

When you are happy with the text you have typed on the command line, press the ENTER key. It is only then that DOS will try to interpret your command or message. If you had typed the text above, DOS will issue the message:

        Bad command or file name

You have to type a valid command for DOS to obey and execute it. You will learn most of the important DOS commands later in this book. Once you have learned these, you will feel much more confident about your PC and use it more effectively.

Instead of typing a DOS command, if you had typed a program name, DOS will automatically load that program in memory and run it.

Command structure

The basic structure or format of all DOS commands is the same. There are up to three parts to a full command. These are:

COMMAND	PARAMETERS	OPTIONS

For example, the DOS command:

```
DIR A: /W
```

will display a directory of files on your disk. The 'A:' parameter indicates that you want to see the files in your A floppy disk. The '/W' option (sometimes referred to as a switch) will display the directory in wide format, occupying up to five columns.

We will discuss the DIR command in detail later, under the File Management chapter. For now, it is enough to understand just the basic format of DOS commands.

The parameters and options are not always compulsory. The DIR command on its own will display a file list from the current disk in a single column. For some DOS commands parameters are essential, because without any, the command cannot work. For example, to COPY a file you need to specify the file to copy and where to copy it.

Basic Commands

Here are some basic DOS commands you can type, after powering up your PC:

From the Command Prompt

VER

If you are not sure which version of DOS you have, VER will tell you.

DATE or TIME

There is an internal clock in your PC keeping track of the date and time. Type either of them to check if they are set correctly. You will have an option to reset them if necessary.

HELP *command*

The HELP command on its own will display DOS commands alphabetically with a brief description on each one.

If you provide a specific DOS command as a parameter to HELP, more detailed information about that command, together with different parameters and options available, will be displayed.

Cont'd....

CLS

This will simply clear the screen.

Internal & External Commands

There are two types of DOS commands: internal and external. Internal commands are all contained within a file called COMMAND.COM. This file is loaded automatically into memory when DOS is loaded. Examples of internal commands include:

COPY, DEL, DIR, TYPE

These commands can be issued from any disk drive or directory because they are in memory.

External commands, however are not in memory to start with. They reside as separate files on your disk; one for each command. When you issue an external command, the relevant file has to be located and loaded into memory from disk - just like when you want to run a program. Examples include:

BACKUP, CHKDSK, FORMAT, UNDELETE

Both, internal and external commands will be described

later in this book. Also, Appendix B lists all major DOS commands and tells you whether they are internal or external.

The DOS Shell

The DOS Shell is an easy-to-use menu driven interface between you and DOS. It was introduced in version 4.0 by Microsoft and improved in version 5.0. Many of the common DOS commands can be issued easily from the Shell.

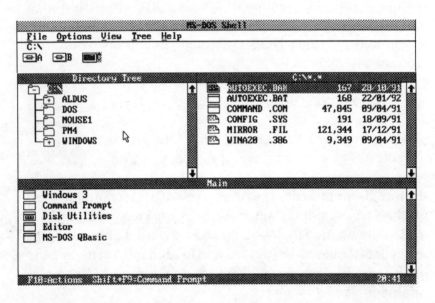

In short, the DOS Shell is a Graphical User Interface (commonly abbreviated as GUI - pronounced 'gooey'). It replaces the Command Prompt and the Command Line. Instead of the almost blank screen and the Command

Prompt, a full screen is displayed with names of common applications, files and directories (see later). These are all prefixed with little *icons* (or pictures) that give clues to what the items may contain. It also provides 'pull-down' menus and mouse support to make things a little easier.

The greatest advantage of using the Shell is that you will not have to memorise or type commands at the Command Prompt. However, the Shell will not allow you to perform all functions available within DOS. Therefore, there is a facility within the Shell to allow you to temporarily exit to the Command Prompt. Here you can issue a command or two by typing in the traditional way.

When you install DOS (see Appendix A) you will have the option to run the Shell automatically on startup. If you do not choose this option, you can still activate the Shell by typing:

        DOSSHELL

We will look at how to perform basic functions within the Shell in the next chapter.

Shut Down

Finally, before we leave this chapter let us briefly cover the proper way to switch off your computer.

First exit from applications that you may have been using,

like the word processor, accounts etc. If you are in the Shell, choose Exit from the File menu or press F3.

Then, switch off your printer and any other peripherals that you may have been using. Also, remove any floppy disks that may still be inserted in your drives.

Now you can switch off the power button on the PC.

Using the **DOS Shell**

This chapter will introduce you to using the DOS Shell. Skip this section if you have not installed the Shell, or you have an older version of DOS, or if you simply do not intend to use the Shell.

For the rest, the MS-DOS 5 Shell provides an easy and convenient way of using DOS. Whilst reading this chapter, and the subsequent ones, try using the techniques and commands described on your own PC - this really is the best way to become proficient in DOS.

When the DOS Shell is loaded on your system, you should see the following main screen:

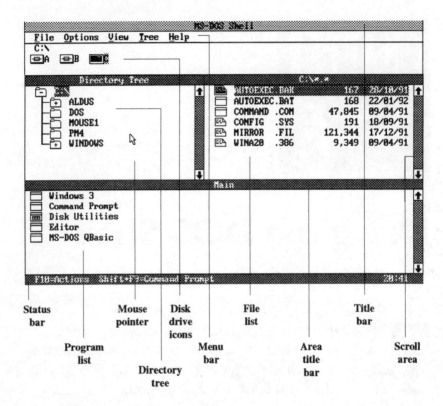

You will see three different areas within the Shell. They are, starting from upper left, Directory Tree, File list to the right, and Main near the bottom.

The easiest way to access a particular area is to click anywhere inside it with your mouse button. If you do not have a mouse, you can press the Tab key on your keyboard to toggle between the three areas. You will always know which area is selected because only one Area title bar is highlighted at any time.

Directory Tree

In this area you can see the structure of all directories. Directories are logical sections on the disk to store information or files. Therefore, you may decide to have a directory for all your word processor documents and another one for spreadsheet files. The wordprocessor directory may consist of other subdirectories, say one for storing all your letters, and another one for your reports. The wordprocessor software could remain in the main directory. We will cover directories in much more detail later in the book.

For now, it is sufficient to understand how the Shell displays directories. The small boxes in front of the directory names are called folder icons. If there is a + symbol inside the folders, you can click on it with your mouse button to see and expand the particular directory into sub-directories. Hence it is called the Directory Tree.

File List

The File list area will display all files contained within a particular directory or sub-directory selected in the Directory tree. To select a directory, click on it with the mouse or use the cursor arrow keys on your keyboard.

Main area

The Main area at the bottom of the screen lists programs that may be used frequently. Double-click on any one of them with your mouse (or select using arrow keys and press Enter) to execute or run the program. Just after you install DOS 5 Shell, you will see:

Command Prompt. Allows you to temporarily go to the command prompt. Here you can enter DOS commands not supported within the Shell. To get back into the Shell, just type:

```
EXIT
```

Editor. This is a text editor used to create or edit files. These may include important DOS files like the Autoexec.bat or Config.sys (see later).

MS-DOS QBasic. You will be able to write your own programs using this Basic programming language.

Disk Utilities. Consists of several different programs. You will be able to Format disks, Copy and Backup files, even Undelete files that have been deleted previously.

If you use a particular program often enough, like a wordprocessor for example, you can create a program group/item of your own to appear here (see later on how to do this). Then, every time you want to use the wordprocessor, simply double-click on this entry.

You can also run several programs simultaneously in the Main area. This is achieved by the new DOS 5 feature called the Task Swapper. This is discussed in detail in Chapter 9 - Working with Programs.

Scroll areas

All the three areas just described have scroll areas to the right. These allow you to scroll up or down when the information to display cannot fit into the small area reserved. Just click on the up-arrow or the down-arrow to scroll gently in either direction. Alternatively, click anywhere between the two arrows to scroll directly to that part of the list. You can also scroll by using the arrow keys and PageUp, PageDown, Home and End keys.

Disk drive icons

These are just above the Directory Tree. You should see disk drive C highlighted by default. To access or use other drives, just click on it with your mouse or press Ctrl-A to access drive A, Ctrl-B to access drive B and so on. Once a drive is selected, you can select other adjacent drives by using the left or right arrow keys.

Menus

Above the Disk drive icons there are five pull-down menu options. These allow you to perform various commonly required tasks. To use them, just click on them. You can also access the menus by pressing F10 or the Alt key. This will first just highlight the File menu - use the arrow keys to access other menu options and then press Enter to see the pull-down menu expanded. You can also press Alt and the first letter of the menu option, say Alt-V, to access the View menu directly. Once you have your pull-down menu, you can select a function from it by clicking on it with a mouse, using the Up or Down arrow keys followed by Enter, or just press the underlined letter of the function you want to perform. If you have selected the wrong menu or function, press the Esc key to backout. Many of the functions or commands will be discussed in the chapters to follow. However, the basic options are:

File. Enables you to manage files (copy, delete, rename), run programs and even create new directories to store files. Sometimes, some options from the pull-down menus are dimmed. If you have a colour screen, you may have them displayed in a different colour (see Changing the display). These options cannot be selected because you have to do something else first, before they can work. For example, if you have not selected the File list area and highlighted

```
Open
Run...
Print
Associate...
Search...
View File Contents    F9

Move...                F7
Copy...                F8
Delete...              Del
Rename...
Change Attributes...

Create Directory...

Select All
Deselect All

Exit                   Alt+F4
```

one or more files, options like Move, Copy, Rename and so on, will be dimmed because they all need files as a pre-requisite. Also, the File menu looks completely different when you are in the Main program area. Try it and see.

Options. This enables you to tailor the DOS 5 Shell the way you prefer to work. It allows you to change the display (see later), choose whether you want to be prompted to confirm deletion of files and what information you prefer to see displayed about files.

View. Allows you to split the screen to display two file lists (so you can compare the entries from two disks say), display program list, file list or both and re-display the screen to show new entries.

Tree. Shows you the directory structure. You can "expand" or "collapse" directories or sub-directories. The Tree menu option is not displayed when the Main area is active because it is not relevant.

Help. Displays online help on your screen (see later).

Dialog boxes

Some of the functions you may select from the menus will present you with a dialog box. If you see ... next to a menu function, a dialog box is usually displayed on selection. The ... indicates that further information will be required. For example, if you select **Create Directory ...** from the File menu you will get:

```
┌─────────────────┤ Create Directory ├─────────────────┐
│                                                       │
│                                                       │
│   Parent name: C:\                                    │
│                                                       │
│   New directory name. .    ┌──────────────────┐       │
│                            │_                 │       │
│                            └──────────────────┘       │
│                                                       │
│                                                       │
│                                                       │
│       ▒▒▒▒OK▒▒▒▒       ▒▒▒Cancel▒▒▒       ▒▒▒Help▒▒▒   │
│                                                       │
└───────────────────────────────────────────────────────┘
```

Here, you will have to type the name of the new directory you want to create. You can click on cancel or press the Esc key if you have changed your mind and do not want to create a directory.

Sometimes, a dialog box will make you choose an item from a list. For example, to choose a colour scheme for your display. At other times, you will be able to make several choices rather than just one. This type of dialog box is sometimes called a check box. For example, you can select as many or none of the options in the box below:

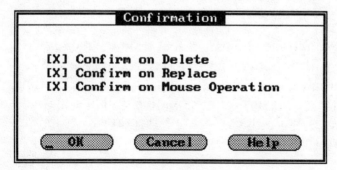

```
┌─────────────┤ Confirmation ├─────────────┐
│                                           │
│                                           │
│    [X] Confirm on Delete                  │
│    [X] Confirm on Replace                 │
│    [X] Confirm on Mouse Operation         │
│                                           │
│                                           │
│     ▒▒OK▒▒       ▒▒Cancel▒▒    ▒▒Help▒▒    │
│                                           │
└───────────────────────────────────────────┘
```

Click between the square brackets to select a particular option. An '**X**' will appear to confirm your selection. Alternatively, you can press the space bar on your keyboard to achieve the same.

Changing the display

If you go into the Options menu you will see an item called Display. Select it to see a dialog box of screen modes:

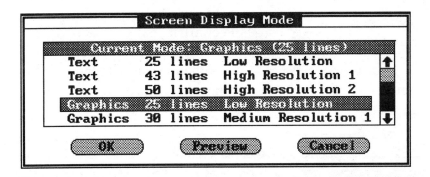

Select either one of the text modes or graphics mode. You can preview the display chosen. If you like it, then click on OK or press Enter.

If you have a colour monitor, you can also choose Colours from the Options menu. Select and preview the colour you like from the scrollable list in the same way as you did with the Display dialog box.

Help

There is an online help facility with your DOS 5 system that can save you time looking up the relevant information in the reference manual. Click on the Help menu with your mouse or just press Alt-H to activate the Help system.

Choose Index for a listing of all Help topics, Keyboard for key-combinations to use with the Shell, Shell Basics to learn and confirm many of the features covered in this chapter, Commands to get help on specific menu commands and Procedures to obtain more detailed instructions on how to perform various functions.

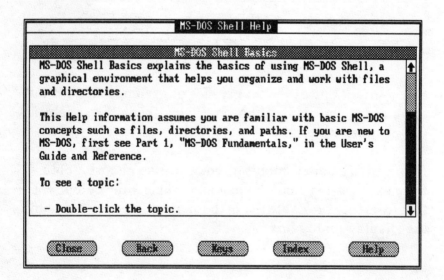

Using Help will teach you how to use the Help system itself and About Shell will show you the version number and the Microsoft Copyright.

If you highlight a menu or a specific command within it and press F1, you will get help specifically on that subject. This is called *context-sensitive help*.

Floppies & Hard disks

The 'D' in DOS stands for Disk. Most DOS commands operate on disks. They access disks to read programs and to manipulate files or data. Therefore it is important to cover some essential basics about disks before we explore many of the DOS commands.

Disks are used to store programs or data. There are two basic types of disks: Floppy disks (floppies) and Hard disks.

Floppy disks

There are two sizes of floppy disks: 5.25" and 3.50". The 3.50" has become the dominant standard. Most PC manufacturers now offer a 3.50" disk drive as standard.

The 3.50" disk offers better protection with a hard plastic casing. It has a small metallic shutter on it. This is the end that is inserted into the disk drive first. A 3.50" disk drive closes automatically when the disk is inserted completely. You will see a little plastic slider on the top right corner. This is the write-protect hole. If you push it with a ball-point nib to reveal a hole, the disk becomes write-protected. You will not be able to write or change anything on the disk. This is useful to protect data from being accidently over-written. E.g. master disks which you buy as part of your software package should always be write-protected.

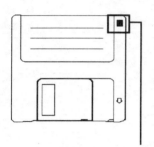

Write-protect hole

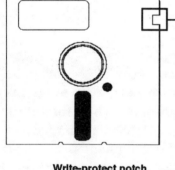

Write-protect notch

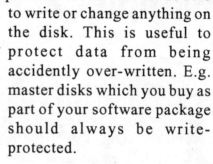

To write-protect a 5.25" disk, it is opposite to 3.50" - you have to cover the small hole (notch) with a sticky tab.

Disk Storage Capacity

The storage capacity of disks can be measured in bytes. One byte is equivalent to one character. A kilobyte is 1024 bytes or characters and it is abbreviated as K or Kb. A megabyte (Mb) is a ~~thousand~~ kilobytes or approximately a million

1024

bytes. The storage capacity is summarised in the following table:

SIZE	CAPACITY	HARDWARE	DOS VERSIONS
3.50" DD	720K	IBM PS/2 30 & compatibles	3.2 or later
3.50" HD	1.44Mb	IBM PS/2, AT or compatibles	3.3 or later
5.25" DD	360K	IBM PC, XT or compatibles	2.0 or later
5.25" HD	1.2Mb	IBM AT or compatibles	3.0 or later

The abbreviation DD stands for double-density disk and HD is for high-density.

Changing disk drives

The first floppy disk drive is usually assigned the letter A to identify it. If you have a second drive it will be assigned the letter B. The letter C is reserved for the hard disk. Other letters are not usually used unless you have additional drives, or if your PC is connected to a network, where you have access to several disks.

It is possible to allocate other letters to represent the standard A,B,C, ... drives with the ASSIGN command. But it is best not to do this as you may have problems running and using some software.

To change from accessing one disk drive to another, using the Shell, just click on the relevant disk drive icon with the mouse, or use tab to highlight one of the icons and then use arrow keys to access the rest. You can also press Ctrl as well as the drive icon, like Ctrl-A for example, to access disk drive A directly from the keyboard.

From the Command Prompt

```
A:
```

will access disk drive A from your current drive. If you want to access another drive, type the letter which identifies it followed by a colon.

To access drive C as A too, type:

```
ASSIGN A = C
```

To check the current assignments:

```
ASSIGN /STATUS
```

To remove all assignments and to go back to the standard assignment, just type:

```
ASSIGN
```

Formatting

Before you can use disks to store information or files you have to prepare them for use. This is achieved by the FORMAT program.

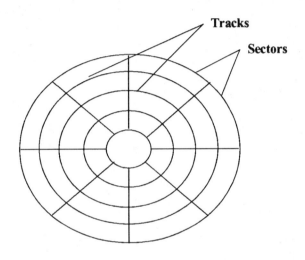

FORMAT will structure the disk into concentric circles called tracks and sectors as shown above. A sector is a pie-slice of a disk.

The number of tracks and sectors on a disk determines its storage capacity. FORMAT will automatically allocate the right number of these, depending on the storage capacity of your disk and the type of disk drive you have.

To format a new disk double-click Disk Utilities from the Main program area in the Shell. Then choose Format floppy disks from Disk Utilities menu.

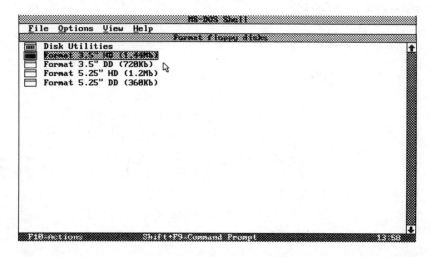

Choose the disk size and capacity and then if you only have one drive applicable for your choice, DOS will automatically prompt you to insert a new disk into the correct drive:

```
Insert new diskette for drive B:
and press ENTER when ready . . .
```

Otherwise type the drive letter followed by a colon. Formatting will commence - taking a few seconds to complete. It will wipe off any information you may have on the disk. So be very careful not to format disks that contain information you still require. In DOS 5 you can use the UNFORMAT command from the Command Prompt to recover files that were lost using FORMAT.

To format a disk in drive B say, type:

```
FORMAT B:
```

DOS will prompt you to insert a disk exactly as it did from the Shell. After you insert the disk and press ENTER, it will display:

```
Checking existing disk format
Saving UNFORMAT information
Verifying 1.44M
        xx percent of disk formatted
```

Then when the disk is formatted, DOS will display:

```
Format complete

Volume label(11 characters, ENTER for
none)?
```

The Volume label is used to identify the contents of the disk. For example you can type ACCOUNTS_92 if you are going to use the disk to backup all your accounts files for 1992.

Cont'd....

Although the VOL label is optional it is well worth using. It serves a similar purpose to sticking a paper label on the disk.

Once you press ENTER after the VOL label prompt, DOS will display some statistics on disk space:

```
1457664   bytes total disk space
1457664   bytes available on disk

    512   bytes in each allocation unit
   2847   allocation units available on disk
```

Volume Serial Number is 045D-1AEA

Format another (Y/N)?

You will also be able to format another disk in the same way here if you are planning to do a few at the same time.

If you want to check the Volume label later for any disk, type:

```
VOL drive
```

To put a Volume label later, or to change or delete it, use:

Cont'd....

```
LABEL  drive:label-text
```

To format a disk and also to transfer DOS system files to it, use:

```
FORMAT    drive: /S
```

It may sometimes prove useful to have DOS on a floppy disk in case there is a problem on the hard disk and you need to boot-up from a floppy.

In DOS 5, COMMAND.COM file is transferred automatically as a system file too. However, if you need some external DOS command files too on the system disk, you need to copy them individually. The most useful ones perhaps are:

```
FORMAT.COM
BACKUP.EXE
RESTORE.EXE
CHKDSK.EXE
```

If you want to transfer DOS to an already formatted disk, type:

```
SYS drive:
```

This has the same effect as the /S option on the

Cont'd....

FORMAT command. Be sure to keep your system disk in a safe place and label it as 'DOS SYSTEM DISK'.

New in DOS 5, you have the facility to perform a quick format in a fraction of the time, if the disk has already been formatted once. The command is:

FORMAT drive: /Q

This is useful if you have disks with old files that are no longer required, and you want to use them for storing new information.

Also, new in DOS 5, you can format a disk to a different capacity. For example,

FORMAT   drive: /f:720

Formats 720K disks in 1.44Mb drives (3.50").

FORMAT   drive: /f:360

Formats 360K disks in 1.2Mb drives (5.25").

This is useful if you want to copy files for someone who only has a lower capacity drive. You cannot format a disk to a higher capacity than your drive and

Cont'd....

you should not really format a higher density disk to a lower one either.

Most of the time, of course, DOS will automatically format disks according to the type of drives you have.

Hard disks

A hard disk is similar to a floppy disk. It is a magnetic coated medium spinning at high speeds, whilst the read/ write head moves between its concentric circles, called tracks. The difference between a floppy disk and a hard disk is that a hard disk spins much faster, contains several magnetic coated platters which are more rigid, and it is enclosed in a metal casing for protection. These differences allow hard disks to offer much more storage and they also provide a much faster response time.

Formatting a Hard disk

Many PC suppliers provide you with the hard disk already formatted. You should not usually have to perform this task yourself - unless you experience a major corruption of the hard disk, or if you have purchased a new hard disk.

The basic procedure is the same as formatting a floppy

disk. However, it will take much longer because there is more to format.

Be careful that you do not accidently format your hard disk (by typing FORMAT C:). You will just get this warning message before it wipes off the whole hard disk:

```
WARNING, ALL DATA ON NON-REMOVABLE DISK
DRIVE C: WILL BE LOST!
Proceed with Format (Y/N)?
```

Check disk

It is good practice to check the status of files and directories on your hard disk regularly. The check disk facility is usually used to check the hard disk, although you can use it to check your floppy disks too.

From the Command Prompt

```
CHKDSK
```

DOS will then display the following information for your own disk:

Volume, Date of Creation and Serial Number
Total storage on the disk
Space occupied by hidden and ordinary files
Space occupied by directories
Number of files and directories

Cont'd....

Disk space still available
Total amount of memory
Memory still available

If you enter:

CHKDSK /F

portions of files that have been separated from their original files will be located. These are called "lost clusters". You will have the option to convert these lost clusters to files. If you do this, sequentially numbered files with an extension .CHK will be created. You can print these files to see if the data they contain is of any importance and if not, then simply delete them to save space on the disk. Use:

CHKDSK /V

to display each individual file as it is being checked. Use:

CHKDSK *drive:*

to check a disk in another drive.

Hard disk Organisation

Hard disks offer much greater storage capability than floppies, as discussed in the previous chapter. It is not uncommon now to find hard disks with several hundred megabytes of storage. However, most computers nowadays have at least 40 or 50 Mb hard disk already built into the system unit.

The problem with so much storage is that it is easy to populate it with so many files that it becomes difficult to find anything. To resolve this problem, DOS provides us with a multi-level directory structure. This is a convenient way of keeping related files or information together. This concept and the commands described in this chapter can also be used for a floppy disk, but it is more common and necessary to use them to keep a hard disk organised.

Multi-level directory structure

A multi-level directory structure is sometimes referred to as an upside-down tree. The root directory is at the top. This is created automatically when you format a disk. You can store files here or create other directories from the root, called sub-directories. Within each sub-directory you can store more files or create further sub-directories. The tree therefore, can be expanded and structured in the way you want to keep your information organised.

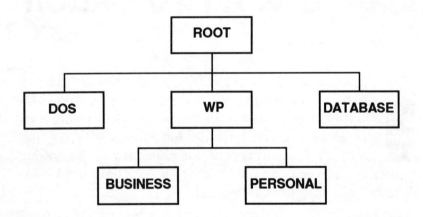

For example, if you bought a word processor, create a WP directory to store all its program files. Then within this directory, create a sub-directory BUSINESS to store all your business communication and another sub-directory PERSONAL to store all your personal letters, as shown above.

Note that most software products can automatically create their own directories when you install them. However, you still need to create sub-directories within these to organise your data.

Pathnames

The concept of pathnames is important in a multi-level directory structure. A pathname is the route DOS needs to know to find a file. For example, if you have a file called LET1.DOC in the PERSONAL sub-directory, the pathname is:

C:\WP\PERSONAL

You need to specify the path by giving DOS all the sub-directory names from the root, in the correct order, to get to the file. You could have another file, also called LET1.DOC in the BUSINESS sub-directory. DOS will always access the correct file because the pathname will be different.

Most DOS commands should have the pathname concatenated with the filename. So for example, if you want to manipulate the file LET1.DOC in some way, or just access it, type:

C:\WP\PERSONAL\LET1.DOC

You can specify just the filename if you are already in the

appropriate directory or if you have previously issued a PATH command.

The path command establishes a link to one or more directories that are accessed regularly, so you can avoid typing the path all the time. A good example of this is establishing a path to the DOS directory itself. Many external commands, like FORMAT, UNDELETE and so on, are program files - they do not reside in memory. Therefore, to use them without having to type the path all the time, just type the path command once:

PATH C:\DOS

This statement usually exists in the AUTOEXEC.BAT file (see later). This way you do not need to type it every time after powering on.

Directory tree

From the Shell you do not have to worry too much about the path. By **expanding** the Directory tree you can access files from any sub-directory by simply selecting the correct sub-directory. Files in it will be displayed in the File list to the right.

If a directory contains sub-directories, there is a little '+' inside the folder relating to that directory. Click on it or just type '+' to expand that directory to one level. The '+' will then change to a '-' and if you click on it or type '-' then

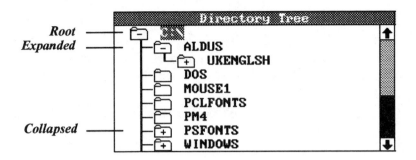

Root ——
Expanded ——

Collapsed ——

the directory will collapse again. You can type '*' to expand a directory to all its levels or type Ctrl-* to expand all directories to all levels.

Note also that the \ (backslash) symbol represents the root directory. You can display the directory tree of a floppy disk by clicking on the relevant drive icon or typing Ctrl-A or Ctrl-B.

From the Command Prompt

Type:

    TREE

This command will expand all directories and sub-directories from the directory you issue the command.

Creating directories

If you want to create a new directory, first hightlight the

directory from which you want to create a new sub-directory from. This is called the parent directory. Your new directory will be a sub-ordinate or a child to that directory Then, choose Create Directory from the File menu:

```
┌──────────────────────────────────────────────────────────┐
│              ▐ Create Directory ▌                          │
│                                                            │
│                                                            │
│    Parent name: C:\                                        │
│                                                            │
│    New directory name. .    ┌──────────────┐               │
│                             │_             │               │
│                             └──────────────┘               │
│                                                            │
│                                                            │
│                                                            │
│     ◖  OK  ◗        ◖ Cancel ◗          ◖ Help ◗           │
│                                                            │
└──────────────────────────────────────────────────────────┘
```

You will see the Create Directory dialog box as above. Just type the name of your new directory in the box. In this example, the new directory will be directly under the root.

┌──┐
│ █From the Command Prompt█   │
│   │
│   You need to first go to the directory from which you   │
│   want to create a new one (see Changing directories).   │
│   Then type: │
│   │
│   MD   dir   │
│   │
│   MD is short for MKDIR or Make Directory. 'dir' is   │
│   the name you want to give to the new directory.   │
│   │
└──┘

Changing directories

When you create a new directory, DOS does not automatically make it the current directory. From the Shell it is easy to change to the new directory. You just click on it from the Directory tree or move to it with the cursor arrow keys.

From the Command Prompt

```
CD dir
```

CD is short for CHDIR or Change Directory. The dir above, can be just the directory name for the next level or a path to the ultimate directory you want to change to. For example, you can type:

```
CD   WP/BUSINESS
```

If you want to move up to WP directory from BUSINESS, type:

```
CD   ..
```

To move straight up to the root directory from anywhere, type:

```
CD \
```

Removing directories

You cannot remove or delete a directory if it contains any files. Therefore, before trying to remove a directory, make sure that you have first deleted all the files within it. Then, from the Shell, just highlight it and press the DEL key. It is as simple as that!

> **From the Command Prompt**
>
> Type:
>
>   RD dir
>
> RD is short for RMDIR or Remove directory.

The Prompt command

> **From the Command Prompt**
>
> When you are moving around different directories at the Command Prompt it is difficult to know where you are in the directory tree structure. The PROMPT command can be used to display the directory path at all times. Type:
>
>   PROMPT pg

Cont'd....

Now, rather than just seeing the disk drive letter, the Command Prompt is changed to display the current directory. For example, when you are at the root directory, the Command Prompt will look like:

    C:\>

The \ again indicating that it is the root directory. If you change to WP directory, the Command Prompt changes to:

    C:\WP>

Changing the directory again to PERSONAL will show:

    C:\WP\PERSONAL>

It is possible to change the Command Prompt in many different ways by using other parameters for the PROMPT command. For example, $d will always show today's date and $t, the current time. Any special name or text after the PROMPT command will be simply be displayed as part of the Command Prompt.

The most useful type of Command Prompt, however, is one that displays the current directory with the

Cont'd....

pg parameter. The PROMPT command with this parameter is usually included in the AUTOEXEC.BAT file (see later).

To revert back to the default Command Prompt, C >, just type the PROMPT command without any parameters.

File Management

iles are basic units of information DOS manages. All your work is stored in a number of files. Some examples of files include word processor documents, spreadsheet forecasts and customer account details. Even software programs you purchase, like Lotus 1-2-3 or WordPerfect, are files and DOS itself consists of files.

The Directory

So how can you find out which files you have on your disk? From the DOS Shell, the File list displays all files in the current directory. If you click or tab on another directory, in the Directory tree area, files from that directory will then be displayed in the File list.

63

DIR

This is short for Directory. It will display files in your current directory. An example of a directory file listing is:

```
Volume in drive C is CS_V0101
Volume Serial Number is 3238-10F7
Directory of C:\

COMMAND   COM   47845      09/04/91   5:00
DOS       <DIR>            04/12/91  10:04
MOUSE1    <DIR>            04/12/91  10:04
DOS1      PCX   33344      31/01/92  20:42
WINDOWS   <DIR>            04/12/91  10:04
CONFIG    SYS     191      18/09/91   8:57
AUTOEXEC  BAT     168      22/01/92  17:06
        4 file(s) 81548 bytes
        35852288 bytes free
```

You will notice from the directory listing that there are five columns of information. The first two indicate the File name. The entries with a <DIR> symbol are not files at all. These are sub-directories of the current directory displayed here.

Then, the size of the file is given in bytes (or number of characters). Finally, the date and time of creation is given for each file.

Naming Conventions

When creating DOS files, either from software products like Lotus 1-2-3 or WordPerfect, or by using the DOS Editor (see later), you must follow certain rules for naming them.

A DOS filename consists of a file name and an extension to the file name. You can only use a maximum of 8 characters for the name and 3 characters for the extension (also known as the file type), separated by a period. Many software packages will automatically create the file type so that it is possible to distinguish which files belong to which software. For example, Excel uses .XLS, Word uses .DOC.

Common file types that DOS uses are:

.EXE (executable) or **.COM** (command). These files contain programs that are executed or run.

.SYS (system) are files that contain information about your system. Usually they describe characteristics of components you can connect to your PC. These are called device drivers (see Appendix C).

.BAT (batch) contains a list of commands that DOS will execute sequentially.

It does not matter whether you use uppercase or lowercase letters in the file name. DOS treats them as being the same.

You can use any letters of the alphabet, numbers and the following special characters to name a file:

_	underscore	&	ampersand
^	caret	-	hyphen
$	dollar	{}	braces
~	tilde	()	parenthesis
!	exclamation	@	at symbol
#	number symbol	'	apostrophe
%	percent	'	grave accent

No other characters are valid in the file name.

Viewing files

The Shell provides several ways of viewing the files you have. You can view most files and the related information from the View menu. For example, Single File list will show:

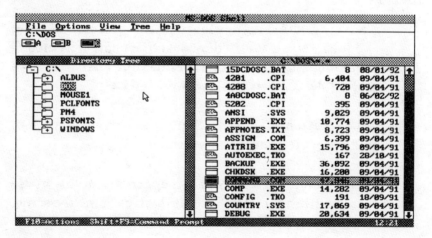

You could choose to see a Dual file list. This can be useful when you are copying or moving files from one disk or directory, to another (these operations are covered a little later in this chapter). Files in both your source and destination drive/directory are displayed at the same time on one screen (sometimes referred to as split-screen display) as shown below:

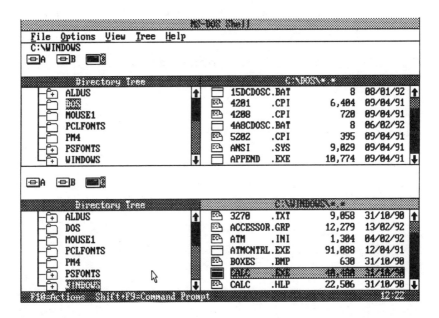

You can select the appropriate file list simply by clicking anywhere in its area.

Also, you will notice that even the disk drive icons are duplicated on the second file list. So you could click on say disk drive A from the second file list to display files from your floppy disk A. Make sure, however, that you have first inserted a disk in drive A.

Both Single and Dual file lists also display the directory tree on the left. You can click on another directory name to see files from it.

You could display files from all directories at once by choosing All Files from the View menu.

You will see that as well as the file name, size (in bytes), and date, this display also shows the time each file was created or changed.

On the left, there is more detailed information. This includes information on the disk and the directory a particular file is in. It shows the total size of the disk, number of files and directories on it, and perhaps the most important is the amount of space still available or free.

This file information changes as you select another file from the File list. You can also see this same file information from other file views. Select a file and then select Show information from the Options menu.

From the Command Prompt

One of the problems you face, when displaying files, is that if there are too many, a DIR listing will quickly list them all, but the earlier ones will disappear off the top of the display. To get around this problem, type:

```
DIR /P
```

/P is an option (sometimes called a switch) on the DIR command. It stands for Page at a time. Once a screen is full with the file list, there is a pause. You will be able to read the details and when you are ready to see the next chunk, press any key.

```
DIR /W
```

/W is another option. It displays files in a wide format of up to five columns. You will not, however, see the size and date/time of creation with this display.

Sorting files

In the Shell, files are usually displayed in alphabetical order. If you want to change this sequence, choose File display options from the Options menu.

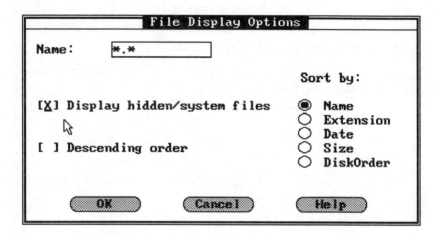

You can click on any sort sequence on the right. Files will then be sorted and displayed in that sequence. They will be in ascending order, unless you click on the Descending order box.

If you select Display hidden/system files box as shown above, these files are displayed too in your file listing. You will see, for example, **IO.SYS** and **MSDOS.SYS** files. These files are part of the MS-DOS operating system not usually displayed in a file listing.

From the Command Prompt

Use the **/o** option in the DIR command to sort files in the required sequence. You have a choice of sorting files in one of the following order:

/on   file name alphabetically
/o-n file name alphabetically, but descending
/oe   extension alphabetically
/o-e extension alphabetically, but descending
/od   date increasing (oldest file first)
/o-d date descreasing (newest file first)
/os   file size increasing (smallest file first)
/o-s file size decreasing (largest file first)

Note that you can combine options in the DIR command. For example:

```
DIR /od /p
```

to display files from the current directory, starting with the oldest and pausing after a screen full.

Changing file attributes

Unlike the normal attributes or characteristics of a file, like size, date and time, which are updated by the system, there are others which you can define and control.

Select Changing attributes... from the File menu. You will then be able to see and change one or more of the following file attributes:

Hidden. File cannot be seen in the file or directory listing. This is useful if you have a secret file that you do not want anyone else to see.

System. System files are also not listed in the file directory. You should not use this attribute. It is reserved for DOS system files only.

Archive. Indicates whether a file has changed since it was last backed up.

Read only. These files cannot be changed. You can only read or display them.

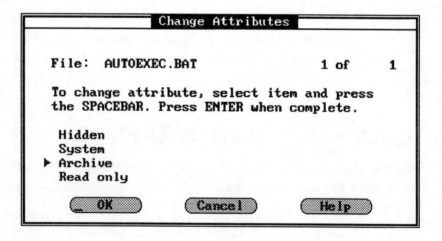

Current file attributes are indicated by a little arrow. To deselect these or to select new attributes, click on the attribute or move to it with arrow keys and press space bar. Choose OK to confirm your changes.

```
From the Command Prompt

        ATTRIB   filename
```

This will display the current attributes for all your files or the specific file named. The display will show file names prefixed with A (for Archive), S (for System), H (for Hidden), and R (for Read only). For example:

```
    A    SHR  C:\IO.SYS
    A    SHR  C:\MSDOS.SYS
    A      R  C:\COMMAND.COM
    A         C:\AUTOEXEC.BAT
```

To change attributes, use the same letters but prefix these with '+' to select the attribute or '-' to deselect it. For example:

```
    ATTRIB   +H   SECRET.DOC

    ATTRIB   -H  +R   SECRET.DOC

    ATTRIB   -A  -S  -H  -R    MSDOS.SYS
```

Contents of files

So far we have only seen which files we have on the PC and their associated information. But how do we read the information within a file?

For most files you cannot really read the contents directly from DOS. This is because many are program files that contain codes that are not readable. Others may be document files, but created using a software product like a word processor or a spreadsheet. These products put control codes in files and so you should use the same products to read them. If you attempt to read these files you will just see unmeaningful gobbledygook.

You can, however, read a pure text file (sometimes called an ASCII file). From the Shell select the file and press F9 or select View File Contents from the File menu.

From the Command Prompt

    TYPE *filename*

See the next chapter, Redirecting Information, to learn how to control the display, if a file is likely to occupy more than one screen.

Selecting files

Many of the functions or commands that operate on files need to have file(s) selected as a pre-requisite. To just select one file, we know that you simply click on it or use the arrow keys to highlight it.

But what if you want to select several files? One technique is called Shift-clicking. This is used to select a consecutive block of files. Click on the first file you want to select. Then, press the

15DCDOSC.BAT		8	08/01/92
17D9DOSC.BAT		8	19/02/92
1A21DOSC.BAT		8	19/02/92
4201	.CPI	6,404	09/04/91
4208	.CPI	720	09/04/91
4A8CDOSC.BAT		8	06/02/92
5202	.CPI	395	09/04/91
ANSI	.SYS	9,029	09/04/91
APPEND	.EXE	10,774	09/04/91

Shift key and click on the last file, still holding the Shift key down. All the files you have chosen will be highlighted.

DISKCOPY.COM	11,793	09/04/91
DISPLAY .SYS	15,792	09/04/91
DOSHELP .HLP	5,651	09/04/91
DOSKEY .COM	5,883	09/04/91
DOSSHELL.COM	4,623	09/04/91
DOSSHELL.EXE	235,484	09/04/91
DOSSHELL.GRB	4,421	09/04/91
DOSSHELL.HLP	161,763	09/04/91
DOSSHELL.INI	18,025	11/03/92

If you want to select non-adjacent files, use Ctrl-click. Whilst pressing and holding down the Ctrl key, click on files required from the File list.

If you want to select files from other directories, choose Select Across Directories from the Options menu.

From the Command Prompt

From the Command Prompt it is not as easy. You cannot pre-select files as you can from the Shell. To have a command operate on several files, you have to use *wild cards* as part of the filename.

Wild cards are special characters which can represent any variable number of characters (*) or any single character (?). For example, DOS?.DOC can represent the following files:

>   DOS1.DOC
>   DOS2.DOC
>   DOS3.DOC

But DOS10.DOC will not be selected. However, DOS*.DOC or DOS??.DOC will select it. You can use wild cards in the name and the extension part of the filename.

Searching for files

Wild cards can also be used from the Shell. For example, to search for a particular file. Choose Search from the File menu. A dialog box, as shown below, will be displayed.

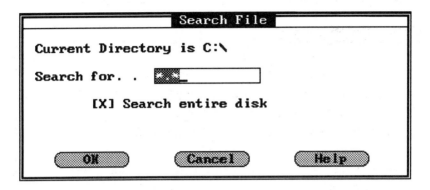

Type any characters of a filename (including extension) that you know. Fill the rest of the name with an * or ?. For example, if you know that your file starts with CUST, type CUST*.* or CUST*.DOC if you know the extension too. Type as much as you know. *.* will search for all files and it is of little use. If you select, Search entire disk, it may take a long time. It is best to narrow down the directories the file may be in, and then select each directory in turn from the Directory tree, before you invoke the search function.

Copying and Moving files

Copying and moving files is a frequent requirement for all users. There are two basic ways of performing these operations using the Shell.

The first one is by using the pull-down menu. Highlight a

file or group of files to be copied and select Copy from the
File menu.

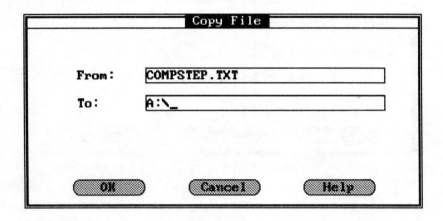

Specify the destination in the "To:" box. You can specify
any disk drive and/or directory here. Click OK to start the
copy operation.

To Move files, the operation is exactly the same as Copying,
except choose Move from the File menu. The only difference
between the two operations is that Copy will leave the
original file there and create a second copy in another disk
or directory. Move will delete the original file after it has
been copied to the new destination. So only one copy of the
file exists if Move is used.

You can specify another file name in the destination box
for the file you are copying or moving. This gives you the
advantage of renaming a file as well as copying/moving in

the same operation (or use the REN command, see later).

The second method of Copying or Moving files is easier and more intuitive. Select a file or a group of files from the file list. If you press the Ctrl-/ keys, it is possible to select all files as shown in the example below. Then, if you want to move all these files to say floppy disk A, click anywhere in the file list and hold the left mouse button down after having made a selection of files to copy. Then, drag the mouse pointer to drive A icon near the top.

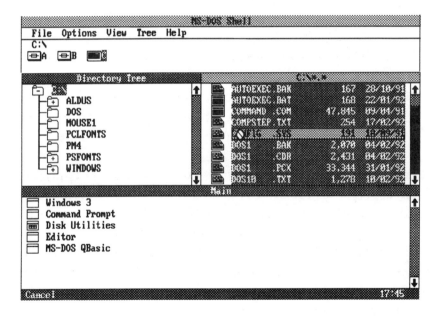

You will see the mouse arrowhead change to and as you drag the mouse over the Directory tree it changes to .

You will be asked to confirm the mouse operation. Then, files will be copied one at a time to your destination. A box showing the status will appear on your screen too.

```
Copying file: COMPSTEP.TXT    4 of    32
```

To Move files instead of Copying, follow the same procedure except hold down the Alt key as you drag the mouse pointer from the file list to a disk drive icon or a directory name.

The only problem with the above procedure for copying/ moving files is that you cannot go to a destination you can not see. For example, how would you copy or move a file to a directory within disk A?

You have to first display a Dual file list. Display the directory tree for disk A in the second file list and then follow the same mouse-dragging procedure.

There is, however, a slight difference. Instead of Copying, you will Move files when dragging the mouse pointer between two file lists. If you want to specifically Copy, then hold down the Ctrl key as you perform the mouse operation.

From the Command Prompt

Files are copied with the COPY command. The format of the command is:

```
COPY from to
```

For example, to copy a file named COMPSTEP.TXT from your hard disk drive C to a floppy disk A, type:

```
COPY COMPSTEP.TXT A:
```

This assumes that you are issuing the COPY command from drive C and from the appropriate directory. If you are not, prefix the filename with the path or change the drive/directory before issuing the command, as described in the last chapter.

If you want to copy and rename the file in the same operation, type:

```
COPY COMPSTEP.TXT A:\COMPSTEP.DOC
```

You will now have a copy of COMPSTEP.TXT file on your A disk, but with a .DOC file extension.

To copy several files, wild cards can be used. For example, to copy all COMPSTEP files, regardless of extension:

Cont'd....

```
COPY  COMPSTEP.*  A:
```

Copying files to another directory, say the DOS directory, is achieved by:

```
COPY C:\COMPSTEP.TXT   C:\DOS
```

This will copy your file from the root directory to the DOS directory within the same C drive.

There is even a way of creating new files quickly using the COPY command. If you want to try out some of the examples given here by creating COMPSTEP.TXT file, type:

```
COPY CON COMPSTEP.TXT
```

CON is short for console or keyboard. This command will copy whatever is typed on the keyboard to a new file called COMPSTEP.TXT.

Type whatever you want after issuing this command and then when you have finished, press F6 or Ctrl-Z (^Z will be displayed on the screen) followed by the Enter key.

Renaming files

If you want to just rename a file without making a copy of it too, first highlight the file you want to rename from the Shell. Then select Rename from the File menu. A dialog box displaying your current filename will appear. Type the new filename in the New name box and press Enter or click on OK. Your file is now renamed to the new name specified.

From the Command Prompt

The basic format of the command to rename files is:

REN *oldfile   newfile*

For example,

REN   COMPSTEP.TXT COMPSTEP.NEW

REN   COMP*.* COMPBOOK.*

REN   CUST92??.DOC CUST92.OLD

Deleting/Undeleting files

To delete a file or a group of files, highlight them in the file list and then select Delete from the File menu. You will see a dialog box asking you to confirm deletion if you have

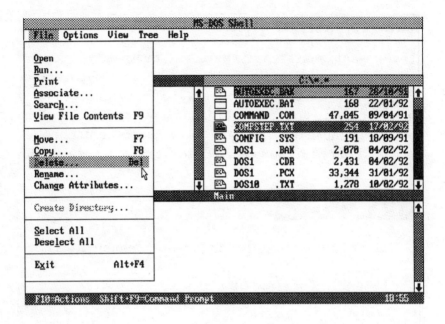

kept the default **Confirm on Delete** status ON (as shown in Chapter 3 under Dialog boxes). It is recommended that you keep this option on to provide a safety net to avoid accidently deleting files you really had no intention of deleting.

There is another, more secure way of ensuring that important information is not lost for good. This is achieved by the UNDELETE facility. But before we look at this you must have the MIRROR program activated. This can only be done from the Command Prompt.

MIRROR   C:/TA/TB/TC

The above command will keep track of files deleted in drives A, B and C. The MIRROR command is an external DOS command. It must therefore be loaded into RAM like any other program and it is also lost when the machine is switched off.

To have the MIRROR command active all the time, include it in the AUTOEXEC.BAT file (see later).

To un-install it, type:

MIRROR   /U

When a file is deleted, it is never physically erased from the disk. Only the entry for the file and where it is stored in the disk is removed from the File Allocation Table (FAT).

Therefore, it is possible to undelete a file as long as you do it immediately after a file is deleted by mistake. It is especially important to avoid creating or changing other files before the UNDELETE command is issued.

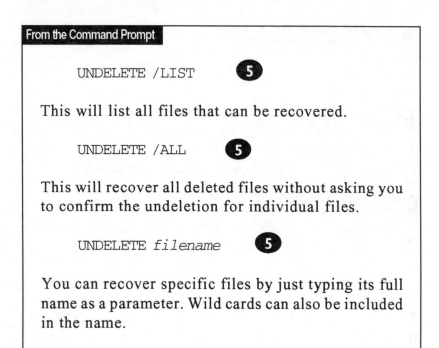

From the Shell, select Disk Utilities from the Main program area by double-clicking on it and then select Undelete:

In the Parameters box type in one of the three parameters given in the Command Prompt section (/LIST, /ALL or filename).

Printing files

To print files in the Shell you must first run the PRINT.COM external DOS command from the Command Prompt.

```
From the Command Prompt

        PRINT
```

Then you will be able to print one or more files by selecting them first and choosing Print from the File menu. Note that you can only really print text files.

Most other files should be printed from the software they were created in. These include word processor, spreadsheet and graphics files.

```
From the Command Prompt

        PRINT filename

        COPY filename  PRN
```

The latter command copies a file to the printer.

Redirecting Information

aving covered basic file management, we can go a stage further. This chapter is about redirectional commands in DOS. These are usually regarded as advanced commands and therefore, are not available directly from the Shell. However, these are not really that difficult, as you will learn. Redirectional commands are generally issued from the Command Prompt.

Basic Redirection

Normally, you issue DOS commands from your keyboard. The keyboard is also called an input console, or CON as far as DOS is concerned. The output from the command is displayed on your monitor (or output console, but again just CON to DOS). Redirection is changing this norm.

From the Command Prompt

For example, the output of the DIR command can be redirected to the printer instead of the screen by:

```
DIR > PRN
```

The > (greater-than) symbol is used for redirection. Make sure that the printer is ON before you issue this command.

You can even redirect the directory list to a file by:

```
DIR > MYFILES.TXT
```

The file will be created automatically if it does not exist. If it does exist, the information in it will be over-written with the latest directory list. To avoid this, use >> (two greater-than) symbols:

```
DIR >> MYFILES.TXT
```

New information will now be added to whatever was in the file, rather than replacing it.

If you want to use your printer as a typewriter and print text on it as you are typing, redirect your input console directly to the printer:

```
COPY CON PRN
```

Cont'd....

After issuing this command, everything you type will echo to the screen and also get printed straight away. To finish, press F6 followed by the Enter key.

You could also print a file, using the COPY command rather than the PRINT command:

```
COPY CUSTLIST.TXT PRN
```

You can use LPT1 instead of PRN to address your first printer.

Apart from the basic redirection, there are two groups of redirectional commands, known as filters and pipes.

Filters

We can use the analogy of the water system to understand filter commands. If you want to purify water in a pipe, you would use a filter to eliminate undesired substances or to extract clean water. Similarly, DOS uses filter commands to modify or select information, as required. The main filter commands are: SORT, FIND, and MORE.

The SORT command sorts a file alphabetically, thereby changing it (or filtering it). FIND can look for certain text in files. It will only output lines from a file that match the text. MORE is a little less obvious. It ensures that output from a command or a file is displayed a page at a time. It puts the word 'MORE' at the bottom of the screen after a screen-full of output is displayed, if there is more to come. You have to press a key to continue the display. It effectively filters the ouput into screen-lots and adds 'MORE'.

From the Command Prompt

```
MORE < CUSTLIST.TXT
```

This will redirect the contents of the file to the screen. Notice that the redirection symbol is pointing in the opposite direction to that described earlier. It always points in the direction the information is flowing.

```
FIND "W1" < CUSTLIST.TXT
```

Part of the postcode, "W1", is being searched for in this file.

```
SORT < CUSTLIST.TXT
```

The file, CUSTLIST.TXT, gets sorted alphabetically. Since the output is not redirected, it will be displayed on the monitor. You can send the output to the printer by:

```
SORT < CUSTLIST.TXT > PRN
```

Pipes

If you want water to flow from one system to another, you can connect a pipe between the two systems to redirect the flow of water. In the same way, the DOS pipe, symbolised by | can redirect output from one DOS command to another.

```
    DIR | SORT
```

The output from the directory command is piped to the SORT command filter. It is then displayed on the screen because it is not redirected anywhere else.

```
    TYPE CUSTLIST.TXT | MORE
```

The contents of the file is piped to MORE so that it is displayed a screen at a time.

You can combine several of these commands. For example:

```
FIND "MALE" < CUST | FIND "W1" | SORT > PRN
```

This will find all male customers from the CUST file, feed the result to the next selection, which will only keep those male customers who live in the 'W1' postal area. Then, these are all sorted alphabetically and finally printed.

Backup Procedures

Protecting the information you have on your PC cannot be over-emphasised. Sooner or later you will encounter a problem and may loose work which has taken hours, days or even months to compile.

The most common cause of data loss is human error. You can easily type the wrong command and wipe off things you did not mean to. Next comes data loss because of hardware or software failure. If your computer suddenly packs up when you are in the middle of an application, some files may get corrupted. A bug in a new release of a software package you bought, or a virus you may have inherited by copying files from outsiders, may also do strange things to your data. The last and often overlooked case is when the data storage media itself is damaged or lost by theft or natural disasters such as fire or flood.

To avoid losing data completely in such incidents, you have to get into the habit of taking regular backups. There are special backup software products you can buy to achieve this. But you do not strictly need these because DOS provides adequate facilities to secure your files.

There are several ways DOS can help depending on your needs. You can use COPY or XCOPY commands, Disk Copy, or Backup and Restore. We will discuss each method in turn.

Copy and Xcopy

The COPY command can be used to copy individual files, groups of files or directories. It has already been discussed under the File Management chapter.

From the Command Prompt

XCOPY can be thought of as an eXtended version of the COPY command. You can use it in the same way as the COPY command but there are additional options available:

```
XCOPY C:\WP A: /S /E
```

/S option will also copy all sub-directories under WP, but not if the sub-directories are empty. /E will copy

Cont'd....

even empty sub-directories so that the original tree structure can be maintained completely.

    XCOPY C:\WP A: d:31-12-92

only copies files that were changed on or after 31st of December 1992.

    XCOPY A: C:\NEWPROG

will copy all files from the A disk to NEWPROG directory on drive C. The unique feature is that even if NEWPROG directory does not exist, XCOPY will create it first and then copy.

    XCOPY C:\WP A: /M

will only copy files to A if they have been modified since the last BACKUP or XCOPY operation. The files are also tagged so that next time they will not be overwritten unless they are different. Use the /A option with XCOPY next time to only copy changed files.

Disk Copy

If you want an exact copy of the files in a floppy disk, Disk Copy is probably the best command to use. It is ideal for

making backup copies of software master disks you have
purchased.

To use Disk Copy, select Disk Utilities from the Main Shell
area and then Disk Copy.

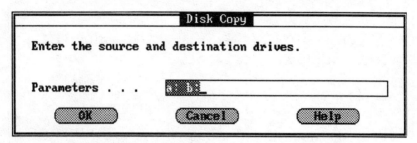

A dialog box with the default parameters of copy from disk
drive a: to b: will be shown. If you only have one drive, it
is possible to type a: a: as parameters. You will be
prompted to insert the source disk to read the files from and
then you will have to swap it with the target disk for writing
the files to.

Note that the two disks must be the same type and capacity.
If the target disk is not formatted, it does not matter
because it will be formatted in the same operation.

From the Command Prompt

```
        DISKCOPY A: B:

        DISKCOPY A: B: /V        5
```

> **Cont'd....**
>
> The /V option will copy, and also verify or check the contents to ensure that they are the same. If you have an earlier version of DOS or if you want to compare the contents of two disks sometime after a diskcopy operation, use:
>
> ```
> DISKCOMP A: B:
> ```
>
> If both disks are identical, you will get the message:
>
> ```
> Compared OK
> ```
>
> You can not use this command if COPY was used to duplicate the same files in two disks. This is because files may have been copied to different tracks on the disk and so the contents will not match exactly.

Backup and Restore

Finally, the Backup and Restore programs are probably the best ones to use for taking backups of large chunks of the hard disk onto floppies, or a very large file which will not fit into just one floppy disk.

These commands are ideal for backing up the whole hard disk onto several floppies. However, you will need a large supply of floppies if you are going to do this. The exact number will depend on the amount of information being backed up and the capacity of your floppies. To work out the number of floppies you will need: divide the number of bytes to be backed up with the storage capacity (in bytes) of one of your floppy disks and round the number up.

For example, to backup 50Mb of hard disk onto 720K size floppies, you will need: $(50,000 \times 1024)/(720 \times 1024) =$ 69.4 floppies.

It is best to have at least 70 floppies for the above example. To find out the number of bytes occupied on the hard disk, use the CHKDSK command. If you are only backing certain files or directories, add the sizes of these files either from the file information display or a directory listing.

If all your floppies are not formatted, don't worry because the BACKUP command will format them too.

To start a backup, select Disk Utilities from the Main program area and then Backup Fixed Disk. You will be presented with a dialog box and the default parameters to backup the whole hard disk. Floppies will need to be inserted in drive A.

```
┌─────────────────── Backup Fixed Disk ───────────────────┐
│                                                         │
│   Enter the source and destination drives.              │
│                                                         │
│                                                         │
│   Parameters . . .    C:\*.* A: /S                      │
│                                                         │
│      ( OK )          ( Cancel )         ( Help )        │
│                                                         │
└─────────────────────────────────────────────────────────┘
```

The /s default option will backup all sub-directories that branch off the main directory specified. In our default settings of course, the main directory specified is the root, indicated by a \.

You can change the default parameters to suit your requirements. Then, once the command is initiated, you will be prompted to insert disk number 1, and then 2, and so on. Large files will be split automatically between floppy disks. You will not have to plan and organise which files were backed-up in which floppies. However, you will have to keep the backed-up disks in the sequence they were used. Label them in sequence, as you use them. Then keep them in a safe place, away from your computer.

Hopefully, you will never need to restore files from these disks. But if your hard disk crashes and most of your files are corrupted, you will need to restore the backed-up files.

Use Restore Fixed Disk option from the Disk Utilities menu. Type in the parameters in the dialog box. They will be same as those used for backup, except in reverse:

```
A: C:\*.* /S
```

The parameters above will restore all backed-up files from drive A to your hard disk C. You will again be prompted to insert disks, one after another. They should be inserted in the sequence labelled.

Use the BACKUP or RESTORE commands followed by the same parameters you would specify from the Shell. So,

    BACKUP C:*.* A: /S

will backup the whole hard disk.

    BACKUP C:\WP*.* A:

will backup just the files in WP sub-directory.

    RESTORE A: C:*.* /S

will restore the whole of your hard disk.

    RESTORE A: C:\WP*.*

will restore the WP sub-directory on your hard disk.

CHAPTER 9

Working with Programs

I n this chapter we will look at how easy it is to setup
and run programs (or applications). The DOS Shell
makes this task very easy and intuitive. We will look
at how to set up new applications in the Shell,
different ways of starting applications, and working with
several programs in memory and switching quickly between
them. The latter is a new feature in DOS 5.

Setting up programs

After you have installed DOS 5 and the Shell, you will see
some programs already set up in the Main area of the Shell.
These are Command Prompt, Disk Utilities, Editor and
MS-DOS Qbasic.

Some of these are Program Groups, like Disk Utilities. Others are Program Items. If you select a group you will not run any program, but another menu with further selection of programs will be displayed.

You can add your own Program Groups and Items to the standard ones that are provided. If you are going to be using a particular program frequently, like Windows or a word processor, it is worth while setting it up in the Main area.

To set up a new Program Group or Item, select New from the File menu on top. You will only see this option if the Main area in the Shell is highlighted or selected first. Also, ensure that you have displayed the group you want to add your new Program Group or Item to. Once you have selected New, you will be presented with a New Program Object dialog box as shown below:

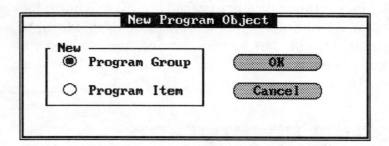

Choose Program Group or Item from the dialog box and then OK. If you choose Program Group, you will get another simple dialog box - Add Group:

```
┌─────────────────────────────────────────────┐
│ ▐          Add  Group          ▌             │
│ Required                                     │
│                                              │
│   Title . . . .    ┌────────────────────┐    │
│                    │_                   │    │
│ Optional           └────────────────────┘    │
│                                              │
│   Help Text . .    ┌────────────────────┐    │
│                    │                    │    │
│                    └────────────────────┘    │
│   Password   . .   ┌──────────────┐          │
│                    │              │          │
│                    └──────────────┘          │
│                                              │
│   ( OK )         ( Cancel )      ( Help )     │
│                                              │
└─────────────────────────────────────────────┘
```

Type in the Title you want to give your Group. Whatever text you type here, will be displayed in the Shell. You can also type a Help message and a password if you want to. The password will stop other unauthorised people using your application. This security check is only available via the Shell, though. Anyone can run your programs from the Command Prompt. Choose OK and you will see the Group title appear in the Main program list.

If at a later date you want to change the title of your Group or the help text and password, you can do so by choosing Properties from the File menu. In order to change the password, you will need to provide the current password. Otherwise, of course, there is no security!

Choose Properties also, to alter details for a Program Item. To add a Program Item initially, select New from the File

105

menu, as you did for a Group. Then choose Program Item from the dialog box to get the Add Program dialog box as shown below:

```
┌─────────────────────────┤ Add Program ├─────────────────────────┐
│                                                                 │
│  Program Title . . . .  [_                                    ] │
│                                                                 │
│  Commands  . . . . . .  [                                     ] │
│                                                                 │
│  Startup Directory . .  [                                     ] │
│                                                                 │
│  Application Shortcut Key      [                            ]   │
│                                                                 │
│  [X] Pause after exit       Password . .  [              ]      │
│                                                                 │
│     ( OK )      ( Cancel )     ( Help )     ( Advanced... )      │
└─────────────────────────────────────────────────────────────────┘
```

Type in the Title as you did for a Group. It will again be displayed in the Shell and used by you to identify and run the program. In the Commands box, type the exact command to start the program (e.g. WORD, WP, EXCEL, 123). You can often follow the command with a filename that you want loaded as soon as you go into that program. e.g. WORD C:\WP\BUSINESS\CUST9212.DOC.

If you do not always want to work with a particular file, but there are many files that you access frequently from a particular directory, then type in a path for that directory in the Startup Directory box. You will automatically access this directory as soon as the program has started. e.g. C:\WP\BUSINESS.

The Application Shortcut Key enables you to switch to this program instantly once it has been started in the Active task list (see Task Swapper later). The shortcut key has to be a 'Alt', 'Ctrl' or 'Shift' key combinations. You cannot use a combination like Alt-F, because the Shell uses it to display the File menu. You can include this shortcut key as part of your title, so that it is displayed, and you will not have to remember it.

To be able to return to the Shell after you exit the program, you need to keep the Pause after exit box selected. The password to the right of it is optional. If you type one in, you will be required to type it in every time before you can run the program. Choose OK to confirm your settings and to set up the new Program Item.

Remember that you can set up as many programs as you want. You can set up the same program with different filenames or directories. Your actual programs are not duplicated - they are just accessed in different ways, from the Shell. You can also delete Program Groups or Items by choosing Delete from the File menu after highlighting the relevant program. Your actual programs will not be deleted - only the entries in the Shell to access them easily, will be deleted.

It is also possible to rearrange Program Group or Item entries, once they have been created. Highlight the entry you want to move. Then, choose Reorder from the File menu. Nothing will happen. But if you select a new location and double-click there or press the Enter key, your initial entry will move there. You can use this procedure to reorder your program entries alphabetically, or put the most frequently used programs at the top.

Starting programs

There are several ways of starting or running programs from the Shell. If you have gone to the trouble of setting up programs in the program list as just described, the easiest way to start a program is to just double-click on its title with the mouse. Using the keyboard, you can highlight the program you want with the arrow keys and then press Enter. If you have set up Program Groups, selecting them will display other Groups or actual Program Items that you can run.

You can also double-click a program file from the File list to run it. They usually have an extension of .EXE or .COM. Another useful technique is to select a file you want to use with your program by highlighting it with the mouse and then drag it, keeping the left mouse button depressed, to a program file, either in the File list or the Program list. Let go of the file icon once it's on the program file. Your program will then start and use the file you just dropped on it. Impressive, isn't it?

Another way to start a program is to just select Run from the File menu and type in the name of the program you want to run. You may also need to type the path to the program if it does not exist in the AUTOEXEC.BAT file (see the next chapter).

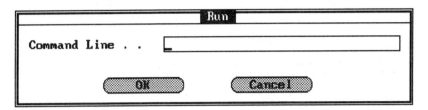

Instead of typing the command to run your program from the Shell, you can choose Command Prompt from the Main Program Group, or press Shift-F9, to temporarily go to the DOS Command Prompt.

From the Command Prompt

Type the name of the program you want to run or execute:

WORD

The above, for example, will run the Microsoft Word program. There should be a WORD.EXE file on your disk, but you do not type the .EXE extension to run the program.

If the program is not in the current directory, you need to also type the path to the directory or have it established prior to issuing the command (as discussed

Cont'd....

before).

To go back to the Shell, type:

        EXIT

If you want to remove the Shell completely from memory and go to the Command Prompt permanently, choose Exit from the File menu or press F3 or Alt-F4.

Once you are at the Command Prompt, you can of course, do more than just run programs. You can use DOS the old-fashioned way by issuing commands from here too.

Task Swapper

The Task Swapper is a new facility introduced in the DOS 5 Shell. It enables you to have several programs running simultaneously in memory and switch between them almost instantly.

To enable the Task Swapper, choose it from the Options menu. An Active Task list is created to the right of the main program group. You can add several programs to this list. Just select programs from the program list or the file list as you normally do to run them (double-click with the mouse or highlight with arrow keys and press Enter), except have the Shift key pressed too. This will not run the programs straight away, but add the program entries to the Active task list.

You can start programs from the Active Task list by double-clicking with the mouse or highlighting an entry with arrow keys and pressing Enter. Once you are running a program, say a word processor, and submitted a print of a long document from it, you can switch to say your spreadsheet, by first pressing Ctrl-Esc from the word processor to get back to the Shell. Then, press Alt-Tab key until the spreadsheet program appears. Let go of the Alt key to select it.

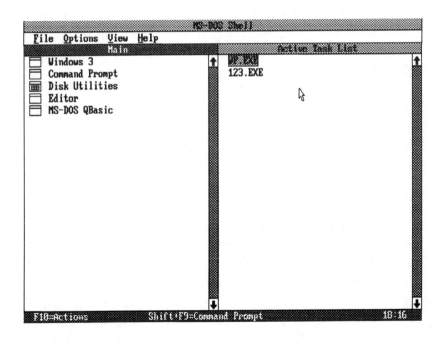

If you run Windows from the DOS 5 Shell, you will not be able to use Ctrl-Esc to switch back to the Shell. This is because Windows also uses Ctrl-Esc key combination to activate its own Task list. Therefore, you will have to Exit Windows to return to the Shell.

Also, if you run memory-resident utilities, also known as TSR (Terminate-and-Stay-Resident) programs, from the Shell, you may experience that the display is not cleared when you return to the Shell. To display the Shell properly again, choose Repaint Screen from the View menu or press Shift-F5.

Choose Refresh from the View menu or press F5 if you return to the Shell from an application, like a word processor, that creates new files or deletes them. The File list and the Directory tree displays will then be updated in the Shell.

CHAPTER 10

Customising your System

You can tailor the way DOS works on your system by modifying two important files. These are AUTOEXEC.BAT and CONFIG.SYS. Everytime you switch on, or boot your PC, DOS reads these files and executes DOS commands within them. Both files usually reside in your root directory.

Most of the time you need not worry about these files. New software you install on your computer usually updates them automatically. It is however, useful to know a little about these files so that you can make your system easier to use and more efficient.

Autoexec.bat

This file is AUTOmatically EXECuted when you start your computer - hence it is called AUTOEXEC. The .BAT extension means that it is a batch file. This is a special type of file where you can group together several DOS commands. When you type just the name of the file (without .BAT), all the commands held will be run sequencially.

Autoexec.bat file can look a little different in different machines. Use the TYPE command to display your version. You can change this file by using EDLIN (stands for a Line editor) if you have an older version of DOS than 5. This is quite cumbersome to use. You can only edit a line at a time. From DOS 5 onwards, you'll be able to use a much better text Editor. To activate it, choose Editor from the Main group in the Shell.

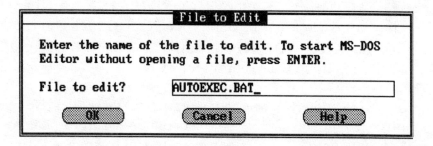

Then, type AUTOEXEC.BAT in the dialog box as shown above. The current text from the file will be displayed and you will be able to make any changes here. To move the cursor in the Editor, simply use the arrow keys or the mouse. You can add new lines by typing them in, followed by the Enter key. To delete characters, press the Del key or Backspace. You can also perform cut-and -paste operations from the Edit pull-down menu. Finally, to save your changes, choose Save from the File menu in the Editor.

From the Command Prompt

To use the same editor from the Command Prompt, type:

      EDIT AUTOEXEC.BAT

Another way to amend your AUTOEXEC.BAT is to use your word processor, but you have to save the file as a pure text file.

An example of an AUTOEXEC.BAT file is:

```
@ECHO OFF
PROMPT $p$g
PATH C:\DOS;C:\WINDOWS
KEYB UK,,C:\DOS\KEYBOARD.SYS
C:\DOS\DOSSHELL
```

@ECHO OFF. This first line just tells DOS not to display the commands or echo them to the screen as they are being executed.

PROMPT pg. As discussed in the Hard disk Organisation chapter, the PROMPT command is used to change the DOS Command Prompt. The pg is the most common parameter used to always display the directory name at the prompt.

PATH. This was also discussed in the Hard disk Organisation chapter. You can specify the directories that you are likely to access most frequently here. If a program you want to execute, or a file you want to access, is in one of the directories specified in the PATH command, you will not need to specify the path to access the file each time.

The order in which you specify the directories is important. If you have the same file name in more than one directory, the version that exists in the first directory in the path, will supersede any subsequent ones you may try and access.

KEYB (KEYBOARD.SYS). This is the keyboard driver. It is used to standardise the keyboard to a particular country. For example, the parameter UK, will allow you to type a £, instead of the default # which is the American standard. The keyboard driver does not have to be in the AUTOEXEC.BAT file - it can be specified in the CONFIG.SYS instead.

DOSSHELL. This will automatically load the DOS Shell after you power up.

If you want to temporarily disable a line from the AUTOEXEC.BAT file, rather than to delete it, just prefix it with REM. This stands for remark. DOS will then ignore it. You can also use REM to write any comments that may be helpful.

Another useful command to have in your AUTOEXEC.BAT is the SET DIRCMD. This defines the way the Directory command will work when you type DIR. For example:

```
SET DIRCMD = /on /p
```

The /on switch will always display the directory list in alphabetical filename sequence and the /p will pause the list whenever a screenful of the directory is displayed.

If you have DOS 5, or a later version, it is wise to tell DOS in the AUTOEXEC.BAT to track deletions. Then, as discussed under File Management, if you accidently delete a file you can use the UNDELETE command. To track deletions in drives A and C only, include this statement:

```
MIRROR C:/TA/TC
```

Also new in DOS 5, there is a useful utility called DOSKEY. It can reduce the number of keystrokes you need to use. You can install the basic utility (without any parameters) by including the line:

```
DOSKEY
```

in your AUTOEXEC.BAT file. Then, it is always there in

117

memory for you to use.

Just some of the useful facilities offered by DOSKEY include:

1. You can access all DOS commands already issued in the current session at the Command Prompt, by using Up and Down cursor arrow keys. When you see the one that you want to use again, simply press the Enter key. If you want to modify the command slightly before re-issuing it, use the Left and Right arrow keys to edit it.

2. Press F7 to display a list of all DOS commands used in the current session.

3. Press F9 to select a command by issuing the relevant command number. These numbers are as indicated in the list displayed, when you pressed F7.

Software installation routines that update your AUTOEXEC.BAT automatically will often save your current version as AUTOEXEC.BAK or AUTOEXEC.OLD. Therefore, if you do not like the changes made to your AUTOEXEC.BAT file, you can rename your version back to the original.

Any changes that are made to the AUTOEXEC.BAT file, either by yourself or by software, will not be effective until you Reset or re-power your computer, or if you re-boot by typing Alt-Ctrl-Del keys.

Config.sys

This is the second important file DOS uses. It stands for CONFIGuration of your SYStem. It allows you to specify new devices like a modem or a scanner you have attached to your PC, so that DOS knows about it. It also informs DOS about the maximum number of files or memory buffers your software applications will require.

Like the AUTOEXEC.BAT file, it may be updated automatically by any new software you install. You can again use the Editor to edit it yourself, and you have to re-boot or re-start your computer to make the changes effective.

A CONFIG.SYS file may look something like:

```
DEVICE=C:\DOS\SETVER.EXE
DEVICE=C:\DOS\HIMEM.SYS
DOS=HIGH
DEVICE=C:\DOS\SMARTDRV.SYS 2048
COUNTRY=044,,C:\DOS\COUNTRY.SYS
FILES=30
BUFFERS=16
```

You will notice several statements starting with DEVICE. These define additional peripherals, like a scanner or a mouse, which have to be installed separately and do not exist on the main system board of your computer. Different devices are defined by specifying the driver name for it in the DEVICE statement. A driver is just a program telling

DOS about the particular device. It usually has a file type or extension of .SYS, or sometimes .EXE. Refer to Appendix C for a list of drivers used by DOS.

Having said this, the first driver in our example, SETVER.EXE, is not for a hardware device. It is used to fool your software applications into thinking that they are using the version of DOS they were designed for. This is important because when a new version of DOS is released, not all your applications, like your word processor, will be updated overnight to use the new version efficiently. This software driver ensures that when you upgrade DOS, your applications continue to work as if nothing has changed.

The next driver, HIMEM.SYS, is used to make more memory available than the standard 1MB. This extra memory, above 1MB, is called Extended memory. We will come back to memory management in a while.

DOS=HIGH will load most of DOS into the first 64K chunk of extended memory (called high memory area).

The next bit is the SMARTDRV.SYS driver. This is used to provide disk cache. It allows more of your program to be stored in memory rather than on disk. This improves the system performance because, it is much faster to access information from memory than from a disk. In our example, the amount reserved for disk cache is 2048 or 2MB.

Now, before we go any further, let us clarify a few memory

management concepts. It is important to understand how DOS manages and uses memory, to make effective use of your computer system.

The story starts from when IBM designed the IBM PC over a decade ago. At that time, they did not think that anyone will ever need more than 640K of memory, or RAM to be more precise.

So, they only reserved 1MB (1024K) memory, from which a maximum of 640K can be addressed and used by programs. The other 384K memory was reserved as video adapter memory, used to display screens. Since, there has never been a great demand for this memory, it remains largely wasted.

As applications demanded more and more memory, a way had to be found to add more memory and for DOS to be able to address it.

One solution was to use extended memory. This is extra memory above the 1MB. If you are not sure whether you have extended memory, type:

From the Command Prompt
MEM
A typical output from the MEM command, assuming

Cont'd....

we have a config.sys as shown in our example, would
be:

```
 655360 bytes total conventional memory
 655360 bytes available to MS-DOS
 592896 largest executable program size

3145728 bytes total contiguous extended memory
      0 bytes available contiguous extended memory
 983040 bytes available XMS memory
        MS-DOS resident in High Memory Area
```

The 655360 bytes of conventional memory is the standard
640K (655360 divided by 1024). From this, 579K (592896
divided by 1024) is the maximum available for any program.
This means that you cannot run a program larger than this
size. The remaining 61K is reserved for FILES and
BUFFERS statements (see later), and for DOS itself.

Then, the next line tells you that there is 3145728 bytes or
3MB of extended memory available. The zero just means
that none of it is being managed at this time. Only 983040
bytes (960K) of extended (XMS) memory is still available.
This is because out of the 3MB total, 2MB is reserved for
disk caching as specified by the SMARTDRV.SYS driver
in our config.sys file. The remaining 64K of extended
memory is taken up by DOS, with the DOS=HIGH statement

in Config.sys. This is the first block of extended memory, referred to as High Memory Area (HMA).

Extended memory is continuous memory that can be accessed, as required. It can be installed on any PC with a 286 processor or higher.

The other type of memory that can be added to your standard 1Mb memory is called expanded memory. Unlike extended memory, it can be added to any PC, regardless of the processor used.

Expanded memory is also different in that it can only be accessed and exploited in blocks of 64K(called a page). Blocks of 64K memory are "paged" in and out of standard memory from a "pool" of expanded memory, as necessary.

The major drawback of expanded memory is that it cannot be used by all software.

Now, if we go back to our example, the next line starting with COUNTRY, sets your machine to the national standard. The code, 044, is in fact the country code for the UK.

The FILES statement specifies the maximum number of files that any particular application will need to have open. It should be somewhere between 20 and 40. Most software will auotomatically increase this number if necessary, on installation.

Lastly, a "buffer" is a bit like disk cache. It is memory area that is used to store information accessed very frequently from the disk. The BUFFERS statement indicates the maximum number of buffers required.

DOS 5 Features and Installation

Quite often, DOS is already installed for you when you purchase a new PC. It is also sometimes customised for you a little, so that you can start using the machine straight away and know that it has been optimised too.

However, you may have a PC without DOS, or more likely, you have DOS but it is an older version and you want to upgrade it to DOS 5. It is possible to buy DOS 5 upgrade from any computer retailer or mail order company. It is the same as buying any software application package. You will receive master disks and a manual.

If you have an older version of DOS, it is well worth upgrading to DOS 5. There are numerous benefits, as highlighted throughout this book. More specifically, DOS 5:

Allows more memory for your applications. It loads itself into the high memory area to leave more of the conventional memory for your word processor, spreadsheet, database and so.

Provides an easy to use, improved Shell. This is a graphical front to the native DOS language. It is particularly appreciated by non-technical users.

Displays online Help. This is available from the Shell or at the DOS Command Prompt.

Includes a full-screen Editor. Replaces the old line editor. You can use it to edit the DOS system files or any other text files of your own. The screen editor is more flexible and easier to use.

Contains the new Task Swapper feature. Enables you to load several programs in memory and switch between them quickly.

Provides DOSKEY. This utility makes it easier to re-issue commands at the Command Prompt.

Can Undelete files. Helps you to retrieve files that have been accidently deleted.

Can Unformat disks. Helps you retrieve information from a disk that has been accidently formatted.

Performs a Quick Format. You can format disks much more quickly if they have already been formatted before.

Has upgraded the Basic Programming Language. The old GW-BASIC has now been replaced with MS-DOS QBASIC. This is included free of charge with version 5.

DOS 5 installation procedure is very straight forward and easy. If you already have an older version of DOS installed, just insert the first disk (labelled Disk 1) and type:

```
SETUP
```

from your floppy disk drive. You will be prompted to press Ctrl-Alt-Del keys to re-boot your system. If you are installing DOS for the first time, just start your computer after inserting the first DOS disk in drive A.

DOS will automatically read the configuration of your system. It will then display settings that you are likely to need. These are: Date and Time, Country, Keyboard, and where to install DOS.

Use the arrow keys to toggle between these settings and press Enter when the one you want to change is highlighted. You may, for example, want to change the Country and Keyboard standards from the default U.S. to U.K. The date and time may also need to be corrected. Most of you will have a hard disk and you will want to install DOS here. It is, however, possible to install DOS to several floppy disks if you want to. Change the default Hard disk setting to Floppy disk for this.

DOS will then prompt you for the directory to install DOS to and whether you want to run the Shell everytime on startup. It is best to accept the default directory, C:\DOS displayed. If you are a complete beginner, then choose to run the Shell on startup too. If you choose NO for the Shell, you can still choose to run it on startup later on, by amending the AUTOEXEC.BAT - add the statement: DOSSHELL.

Once you have provided the basic information required, DOS will start copying files from the DOS floppy disks to your installation drive. It will display a progress bar showing you how much of the installation has been completed:

27% Complete

You will be prompted to insert other DOS disks, as required. The total number depends on whether you are using 3.50'' or 5.25'' disks. Finally, you will get a message telling you when the installation is completed. Remove the DOS installation disk and press Enter to re-start your system.

DOS Commands and Versions

DOS is upward compatible. This means that the version numbers given here, for each command, allows you to use that command in the same version of DOS as well as all future versions. If you have an older version of DOS than that shown here, you will need to upgrade your DOS to use that particular command on your system.

Command	Version	Type
APPEND	**3.2**	**External**

APPEND 3.2 External
Used to specify directories that a program may need, to search for files. Avoids the need to change the current directory.

Command	Version	Type
ASSIGN	**3.0**	**External**

Allocates another disk drive letter to an existing disk drive.

ATTRIB	**3.0**	**External**

Changes characteristics or attributes of files. e.g. "Read-Only" or "Archive".

BACKUP	**2.0**	**External**

Copies files from the hard disk to floppy disks.

BREAK	**2.0**	**Internal**

Allows you to press Ctrl-Break or Ctrl-C to cancel or interrupt the execution of a long program.

CD	**2.0**	**Internal**

CHDIR achieves the same. Used to change to a different directory.

CHCP	**3.3**	**Internal**

Stands for CHange Code Page. This is effectively the character set. For example, CHCP 860 will change the character set your computer uses to Portuguese.

Command	Version	Type
CHKDSK	1.0	External

CHKDSK   **1.0**   **External**
Short for CHecK DiSK. It is used to check your disk space, including how much free space you still have. It also allows you to fix some errors on the disk and displays the amount of conventional memory available.

CLS   **2.0**   **Internal**
Used from the Command Prompt, it CLears the Screen and re-displays the prompt and the cursor at the top-left corner of the screen.

COMMAND   **1.0**   **External**
Lets you run another copy of DOS on your machine. This simply executes the COMMAND.COM program which is used to interpret commands you type at the keyboard.

COMP   **3.3**   **External**
COMPares two files character by character.

Command	Version	Type
COPY	1.0	Internal

Copies files across to any directory, drive or device. You can also use it to rename the file at the same time.

CTTY	2.0	Internal

Stands for Change TeleTYpe. Your standard input device is the keyboard. You can change this to another new device. See Device Designations (Appendix D).

DATE	1.0	Internal

Displays and sets the system date.

DEL	1.0	Internal

Deletes unwanted files. Same as the ERASE command.

DIR	1.0	Internal

Displays a directory of files on disk.

DISKCOMP	3.2	External

Compares two floppy disks for an exact match. Use it to check that the DISKCOPY(the next command) worked.

<u>Command</u>	<u>Version</u>	<u>Type</u>
DISKCOPY	2.0	**External**

Duplicates a whole disk onto another one. Usually used if you want an exact copy of a floppy disk on another. Both disks must be the same size and the same capacity.

DOSKEY	5.0	**External**

A utility which allows you to re-display and re-issue previously used DOS commands from the Command Prompt.

DOSSHELL	4.0	**External**

Loads the easy to use, menu-driven Shell. You will be able to perform many common DOS functions through this interface.

EDIT	5.0	**External**

This is the new full-screen text editor. It is used to edit just text (also called ASCII) files. It replaces the old EDLIN.

EDLIN	1.0	**External**

Line editor used prior to version 5.0. It serves the same purpose as EDIT. But it is not as good.

Command	Version	Type
ERASE	1.0	**Internal**

Same as DEL.

EXIT	2.0	**Internal**

If you started another copy of DOS with COMMAND, EXIT will return you to the original copy. It is also used to return to the Shell, when you have been temporarily working at the Command Prompt.

EXPAND	5.0	**External**

Un-compresses or expands a DOS file.

FASTOPEN	3.3	**External**

Stores the locations of a number of most recently accessed files in memory, so that those files can be accessed much more quickly.

FC	2.0	**External**

File Compare. It is similar to the COMP command, but the output is more useful.

Command	Version	Type
FDISK	**3.2**	**External**

Allows you to partition your Fixed disk (also called Hard disk). Therefore, although you may only have one physical disk, logically, you can divide it into two. Then, use another drive letter (D for example) to access the second drive.

FIND	**2.0**	**External**

Locates a word or several words in a file or a group of files.

FORMAT	**1.0**	**External**

Prepares disks for use.

HELP	**5.0**	**External**

Displays help on any DOS command. You can also just type the command followed by a /? switch to get help on a specific command.

JOIN	**3.1**	**External**

Logically combines the contents of two disk drives fully, or partially through using directories, so that they are treated as one by DOS.

Command	Version	Type
LABEL	**3.1**	**External**

Creates, changes or deletes the volume label on a disk.

| **MD** | **2.0** | **Internal** |

MKDIR achieves the same. Used to make or create a new directory.

| **MEM** | **4.0** | **External** |

Displays all types of memory available on your system: conventional, expanded and extended.

| **MIRROR** | **5.0** | **External** |

Records information which may be required by UNDELETE and UNFORMAT commands.

| **MODE** | **3.2** | **External** |

Used to configure the peripherals (known as devices to DOS), like the printer, modem, screen, keyboard. It can be used to redirect output from one device to another or just to display the status of a particular device.

Command	Version	Type

MORE 2.0 **External**
Controls the display on your screen so that when there is a screen-full of information, an automatic pause is initiated.

PATH 2.0 **Internal**
Used to specify the directories to be searched to find a program that you will want to run frequently. It avoids the need to type the long-winded path name each time you want to access a program, not in the current directory.

PRINT 2.0 **External**
Allows you to print text files. It also acts as a spooler, which means that it will queue print jobs if there are several to print, leaving you free to do other work on the PC.

PROMPT 2.0 **Internal**
Changes the DOS Command Prompt so that it is more useful to you.

Command	Version	Type
RD	**2.0**	**Internal**

RMDIR achieves the same. Used to remove or delete a directory. This will only work if there are no files in the directory you want to remove.

RECOVER	**2.0**	**External**

DOS will try to recover files that for some reason, it cannot read.

REN	**1.0**	**Internal**

RENAME (in full) can be used too. They both rename a file to a new name.

REPLACE	**3.2**	**External**

Updates (replaces) files from one drive/directory to another if there is a match. Ensure that you are using an up-to-date set of files if more than one set exists.

RESTORE	**2.0**	**External**

Copies files that were backed up using BACKUP. This time, files are copied from floppy disks to the hard disk.

Command	Version	Type
SHARE	3.0	External

Reserves some disk space to store control information about files which are going to be shared in a network.

Command	Version	Type
SORT	2.0	External

Sorts the lines within a file alphabetically.

Command	Version	Type
SUBST	3.1	External

SUBSTitutes a long directory name or path with a letter. It will save you time typing a long path name everytime. Avoid using one of your disk drive letters.

Command	Version	Type
SYS	1.0	External

Makes a disk a DOS systems disk by transferring system files to it.

Command	Version	Type
TIME	1.0	Internal

Displays and allows you to change the system time.

Command	Version	Type
TREE	3.2	External

Displays a hierarchy of directories on a disk.

Command	Version	Type
TYPE	1.0	Internal

Displays a file on the screen.

Command	Version	Type
UNDELETE	5.0	External

Recovers a file that has been deleted by mistake.

Command	Version	Type
UNFORMAT	5.0	External

Recovers lost information from a disk you have formatted by mistake.

Command	Version	Type
VER	2.0	Internal

Displays the version number of DOS you are using.

Command	Version	Type
VOL	2.0	Internal

Displays the volume label of a disk.

Command	Version	Type
XCOPY	3.2	External

This is an eXtended COPY command. It provides more flexibility in selectively copying files and directories.

Device Drivers

DOS includes several device drivers. These are programs which enable you to use various peripherals, like a printer, mouse or a modem with DOS. Some device drivers will be installed automatically when you install DOS. Others may be installed when and if you need them. See Chapter 10 - Customising your System to find out how to install device drivers from the Config.sys file. Popular device drivers include:

ANSI.SYS
This is not a hardware device, but it is for software. It allows you to use a series of characters that produce a certain effect on your screen. These characters were developed by the American National Standards Institute - hence its name. Most software does not require it.

COUNTRY.SYS
Customises your machine to the standards for a specific country. This includes the format of the date and time, currency symbol, and the decimal character.

DISPLAY.SYS
Allows you to specify the type of monitor (MONO, CGA, EGA, LCD) so that DOS can control the display. From DOS 4.01 onwards, this driver automatically checks the type of display adapter in use.

DRIVER.SYS
Enables you to use additional disk drives. For example, DOS has a built-in driver to cope with two floppy disk drives. If you need to install a third one, then this driver will need to be installed too.

EGA.SYS
If you use the new Task Swapper facility from the Shell and you have an EGA monitor, this driver will save and restore the display when you switch tasks.

EMM386.SYS
Uses extended memory to simulate expanded memory on 80386 and 80486 machines.

HIMEM.SYS
Makes extended memory available to applications that can use it. That is, it breaks the old 640K sealing that programs were limited to using. It also allows DOS 5 to be loaded in

the first 64K of extended memory, leaving more of the conventional 640K memory for your other programs. You do, however, need to have a 80286 processor or higher to use this driver.

KEYBOARD.SYS
Similar to the COUNTRY.SYS, this driver defines the keyboard to meet the standards for a specific country.

PRINTER.SYS
You can use this driver to change the printer character set for some printers. Usually, you will get a printer driver when you buy a new printer. This will override the DOS printer driver.

RAMDRIVE.SYS
Enables you to set up a virtual disk in memory (or in RAM, to be more precise). It simulates a hard disk, so that instead of accessing the disk, it reads and writes to RAM. Unlike a real disk, when you switch off your machine, everything in RAM will be lost.

SETVER.EXE
Loads a table in memory of programs and DOS versions they were designed to work with. Then, even if you upgrade your DOS, your other programs can access this table and set the version of DOS to be older. This way, they can continue to work as before.

SMARTDRV.SYS

This is used to reserve extended or expanded memory for disk caching. It is much faster to access data from memory, than it is to access it from disk. Therefore, this driver will help improve performance of some programs.

APPENDIX D

Device Designations

A device designation is used to tell DOS which device you want to access. It can be used in conjunction with many commands described in this book. To differentiate a device from a file name in a command, DOS uses the convention of a ':', suffixed to a device name. As with filenames, DOS does not differentiate between upper and lower case letters for device designations.

Device	Description
A:	Floppy disk drive. It is usually the first one if you have more than one disk drives.
B:	Second floppy disk drive.
C:	Hard disk drive.
D:	Second hard disk.

Device	Description
CON:	Short for console. It refers to the keyboard and the screen.
COM1: or AUX:	Communications port number 1. This is a serial port to which you can connect a device, like a mouse. You may also have additional serial ports labelled, COM2: COM3: COM4: .
LPT1: or PRN:	This is your first parallel printer port. If you have more than one parallel printer connected to your machine, you can access the second one via LPT2: , and the third one via LPT3: .
NUL:	This is a dummy device. It is useful to use this to test a command, before using the real device.

Index

U

UNDELETE 85-86, 126. *See also*
    Commands:UNDELETE
UNFORMAT *See*
    Commands:UNFORMAT

V

VER. *See* commands:VER
Versions. *See* DOS:Versions
VOL. *See* Volume label. *See also*
    Commands:VOL
Volume label 45-46

W

Wide format (DIR) 21, 69
Wild cards 76
Write-protect 40

X

XCOPY. *See* Commands:XCOPY

Reader Comments

If you have any comments after reading this book, send them to the author.

You may wish to express your likes and dislikes about this book. Also, send any suggestions on other computer books you would like the author to write.

Please send your comments to:

Harshad Kotecha (Ref: DOS and all that Jazz)
c/o Computer Step
14 Boleyn Close
Warwick
CV34 6LP

You may also want to read ....

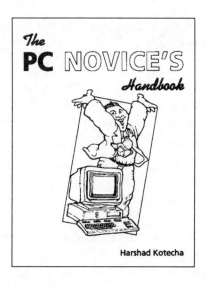

The PC Novice's Handbook demystifies computers in laymen's terms. Specifically written for the UK reader, this is complete guide for choosing, understanding and using personal computers. You will learn about the basic components of the PC and the functions they perform. Then, the book explains what to look for in software and how to purchase the right system. It also simplifies computer communications for you. Includes a list of recommended hardware and software; leading computer magazines, mail order companies, exhibitions and user groups.

ISBN: 1-874029-00-8   PRICE: £8.95